American Paper Son

American Paper Son

A Chinese Immigrant in the Midwest

WAYNE HUNG WONG

Edited and with an Introduction by Benson Tong

University of Illinois Press
Urbana and Chicago

♾ This book is printed on acid-free paper.

Library of Congress Cataloging-in-Publication Data

Wong, Wayne Hung, 1922–
American paper son : a Chinese immigrant in the Midwest /
Wayne Hung Wong; edited and with an introduction by Benson Tong.
p.   cm.
Includes bibliographical references (p.   ) and index.
ISBN-13: 978-0-252-03014-7 (cloth : alk. paper)
ISBN-10: 0-252-03014-1 (cloth : alk. paper)
ISBN-13: 978-0-252-07263-5 (paper : alk. paper)
ISBN-10: 0-252-07263-4 (paper : alk. paper)
1. Wong, Wayne Hung, 1922– 2. Chinese Americans—Kansas—
Wichita—Biography. 3. Immigrants—Kansas—Wichita—Biography.
4. Wichita (Kan.)—Biography. 5. Wichita (Kan.)—Race relations.
I. Tong, Benson, 1964– II. Title.
F689.W6W66   2006
978.1'86004951—dc22   2005011340

Wayne Hung Wong:

For my children—Linda, David, Wilma, and Edward—
and grandchildren—Erik, Kimberly, and Kevin—
so that they may know who I am and where I came from

Benson Tong:
In respect of the intellectual companionship
of Michael Kelly and John Bigelow

Contents

Acknowledgments

A number of generous-spirited people have aided or supported the completion of this work. Barbara Hammond of the Wichita-Sedgwick County Historical Museum, Wichita, Kansas, introduced me to Wayne Hung Wong; she also graciously shared with me some of the notes she compiled on Chinese restaurants in early-twentieth-century Wichita. My former colleague at Wichita State University (WSU), Jay M. Price, shared with me his insights on various themes in public history. I have enjoyed over the years his spirited enthusiasm for and well-rounded knowledge of his subfield. Michael Kelly, former curator of special collections at WSU, offered unremitting emotional support and placed his department's resources at my disposal for an exhibit that served as the genesis for this project. His friendship and professional input have been priceless.

I am deeply grateful to a good number of enthusiastic undergraduate and graduate students who played various roles in the research for this work. Paul Williams took time off to work alongside me in archives in the San Francisco Bay area; his work ethic inspired me. Heidie F. Colucci, John D. Hays, Joshua Yearout, Rana D. Razek, Williams, Isabella Marie Jensen, Theresa L. St. Romain, Teddie G. Barlow, Janice L. Rich, and Benjamin C. Matthaei interviewed Wong and several of his children; they also painstakingly transcribed the lengthy interviews. All of the aforesaid students also assisted in conducting research in local libraries and repositories; their collective efforts unearthed some of the information that serves as the historical context for this autobiography. I am also grateful to all of them for the numerous discussions we had about the autobiography itself. The almost twenty undergraduate students who took my spring 2002 course "Ethnic America in the Twentieth Century" probably never knew, until now, that their stupendous work on an exhibit on race and ethnicity in Wichita allowed me to formulate preliminary ideas about Wong's writing and its place in historiography.

Roger Daniels and an anonymous reader reviewed an earlier version of this manuscript. Their reviews enabled me to sharpen the focus of my interpretive lens on this autobiography; I am indebted to their commitment to rigorous scholarship.

As usual, I am thankful to John for his willingness to amuse himself when I was too busy to pay much attention to him. I am also relieved that at long last I have published an accessible work that he can actually read. I should also point out that John served as my sounding board as I struggled to find a suitable title for this work; for that, I am again reminded of the deeper meaning of our enduring relationship.

Finally, my most heartfelt gratitude goes out to Wayne Hung Wong and his family. Wong's brother, Henjung; Wong's children, Wilma, Linda, and Edward; as well as Wong's wife, Kim Suey, welcomed my students into their lives. So did Wayne. I do not think I will ever meet another more vibrant, open-minded, and self-assured man than Wayne. His life story humbles me; I am in awe of how he triumphed in spite of all the adversities of the earlier years. I thank him for entrusting his memoir in my hands and for the privilege of working on it.

American Paper Son

Introduction:
A Paper Son in the Midwest

Benson Tong

Wayne Hung Wong's *American Paper Son* at first glance is a story of progress, one that reminds a reader of the effervescent "model minority" myth come true. Wong and his family seemingly overcame racial animosity, enjoy phenomenal economic mobility, and are upstanding citizens. So much more, however, lies beneath the surface of a rapid reading. This is in fact a midwestern story of a fraudulent family history, resilient Chinese paper sons,[1] a U.S. serviceman waging the "good war" in his ancestral land, a young war bride and the upbringing of Americanized children, the endless servile labor to reap fortunes in *Gum Saan* (Cantonese for "Gold Mountain"), and, through it all, the enduring transnational ties to the homeland. For sure, various autobiographies have covered one or several of these themes, but never all of them.

So much of Asian American history even until today remains a narrative devoid of names and human depth. Wong's story, however, humanizes what is often a faceless historical saga of invisible forces. Written in a descriptive, sometimes breezy style, the autobiography is replete with anecdotal accounts of both life in China and, more so, in the United States. Not only does it cover a critical period in history when U.S. laws severely limited Chinese immigration—known as the exclusion era—but also the period of family reunification that followed. Wong's memoir also broadens the scope of Chinese American history by shifting the focus away from the West Coast experience, on which much of the existing scholarship has been centered.

The narrative as a whole ties two chronological eras in Chinese American history that are typically studied separately: the pre-1965 period and the era after 1965, the latter year being the turning point for liberalization of U.S. immigration. Wong's expansive story reminds us that the earlier period of split households, immigration networks, an ethnic enclave economy, wartime service, and postwar reunification of families (including the war bride migration) laid a basis for change and continuity in the following era. The shadow cast by the exclusion era's legacy shaped the nature of Chinese American identity and family life in the late twentieth century. Wong's narrative belies the enduring nature of that legacy as he and his family attempted to represent themselves as "Americans" in a land where "American-ness" had been defined by "excluding and containing foreign-ness."[2]

A thought-provoking aspect of this autobiography is the tensions between history and personal memory, between truth and memorialization of the past. (See the appendix for the discussion on the difference between history and memory.) Unlike most Chinese Americans who have written autobiographies, Wong insists, in spite of contrary evidence in his own words, that he had experienced highly limited racial discrimination in his American hometown, Wichita, Kansas.[3] His claim seemingly flies in the face of the often-told tale of victimized Asian immigrants suffering the brunt of "Orientalism."

One of the readers of this manuscript implied that Wong's claim stemmed from his desire to subscribe to the power of the model minority narrative. The overall "progress"-oriented nature of this autobiography also suggests an acceptance of that narrative, one that has enabled marginalized Asian immigrants to find their niche in the dominant society, even though it was and is an ambivalent one. The narrative positions many Asian immigrants and their descendants as "acceptable" Others who will enjoy suitable rewards (educational achievements, economic mobility, and a secure place in society) as long as they continue to meet certain standards such as quiet self-sufficiency, mild-mannered behavior, and acceptance of the existing racialized status quo. By accepting and enacting such a narrative, Asian Americans have believed they could fulfill their "desire to strengthen their status and position in the United States society." In a sense such Asian Americans are trying to attain class ascendancy, which would simultaneously allow them to opt out of the racial hierarchy; their socioeconomic triumph, to quote Ronald Takaki, "offers ideological affirmation of the American Dream."[4] In truth, the model minority narrative masks existing social and economic inequalities that cut across the ethnic line in Asian America.[5]

Because autobiographies are typically self-conscious narratives designed to represent the self from a particular perspective, Wong's claim of having enjoyed a life of relative equality in Wichita has to be considered in that light. Still, the argument that Wong structured his memoir to come across as a model minority member is countered somewhat by Wong's overall understanding of race relations in the United States. Wong never dismisses the discrimination that occurred outside Wichita or within it; throughout this narrative he offers numerous examples of racial prejudice experienced by either himself, family members, friends, or acquaintances. Wong is also well aware of the fact that the exclusion laws were racially motivated and that he was a victim of them. What he does take pains to emphasize is that, overall, his personal experiences *in* Wichita (and, by implication, in the Midwest) had been more positive than negative, which he believed would not have happened on the East or West Coast. Prompting this insistence on his part was perhaps a desire to find acceptance in a place he considered "home," a desire probably strengthened by the fact that he did experience in this city at least subtle hints of racial discrimination (for example, the tensions in the post–Pearl Harbor attack period), and several times a more overt form of rejection (the most notable being the postwar housing discrimination he endured). Perhaps there is also something to be said about the popular, mythical perception of the Midwest influencing Wong's worldview. One scholar argues that the "pastoral idealism" this region embodies metaphorically stands in for the values the republic idealizes, such as wholesomeness, integrity, and egalitarianism.[6]

Wong's understanding of his life mirrors to some degree that of the Korean American immigrant Easurk Emsen Charr in his autobiography *The Golden Mountain: The Autobiography of a Korean Immigrant, 1895–1960* (1996). Wayne Patterson, in his introductory essay to this autobiography, noted that Charr's "experience with racial discrimination is muted in this book," and ascribed that to the general pattern of stoicism in the face of racism exhibited by most first- and second-generation Asian Americans. Patterson also implied that the positive experiences Charr encountered so "outweighed and overshadowed the negative" in the latter's mind that discrimination committed against him was suppressed in his consciousness.[7] Wong can be characterized as one who possesses a stoical mentality. The first version of this work also suggests that Wong's consciousness did block out unpleasant experiences, though there is little evidence of a *conscious* attempt to do so. (See the appendix for a longer discussion of this point.)

Wong's emigration from China to the United States in 1935, at the formative age of thirteen, and the circumstances of that emigration make the story a compelling one. China in the 1920s and 1930s suffered from imperialism, warlordism, a corrupt regime, and socioeconomic turmoil. In this context some Chinese, such as Wong's grandfather, Mar Bong Shui, found a niche in this era of expanding Western influence and sociopolitical change. His import-export business—which most likely had ties to Chinese in the United States—provided him the monetary resources to sponsor the emigration of his son, and indirectly that of his grandson. Unlike the typical portrayal of impoverished peasants desperate to flee socioeconomic upheavals—one that historians of U.S. immigration have described in numerous monographs—Wong's, as well as that of his father's, departure from China reminds readers that some immigrants came from privileged backgrounds and sought either to maintain or improve their standard of living.[8] The Wong family's immigration pattern echoes that of Chinese immigrants described in recent revisionist works by Asian American historians such as Madeline K. Hsu, Yong Chen, and Erika Lee.[9]

Wong's immigration to the United States was also atypical in another respect: he left at the tender age of thirteen to join his father, who needed his labor and probably his companionship. Even though the immigration laws were stacked against family formation and reunification, specifically proscribing the entry of most Chinese women, Chinese American men found other ways to establish some semblance of family life, no matter how distorted it might have been.[10] Typically the men, such as was the case with Wong's paper father, Wong Wing Lock, and several of his male relatives, claimed the birth of a son each time they returned to China for a visit. Over time that enabled them to bring in real sons and also open slots for other kinfolk. Such a "paper son" scheme, as it came to be known, allowed these men to establish and expand the Chinese American community during the exclusion era.[11]

Exposed to the Western world by way of transnational ties forged via family immigration networks, immigrants such as Wong and his relatives were attuned to the concept of immigration. Because Wong's province—Guangdong—had over the centuries been linked to seafaring trade routes, the worldview of the people of this subregion suggested a precapitalist mentality that oriented them toward the outside world.[12] That Wong's grandfather was involved in a business in the British colony of Hong Kong suggests such a mentality.

Such converging conditions explain why some 90 to 95 percent of the Chinese in the United States before 1965 could trace their roots to that province. Perhaps 50 percent of the first-generation Chinese in America hailed from one district alone: Taishan, the same one Wong was born and raised in.[13]

In Taishan the emigration process was facilitated by the assistance of relatives and clanspeople who loaned money and expended time and effort. Wong's (as well as his paper and biological fathers') immigration depended on clanspeople willing to take the risk of jeopardizing their own legal status in the United States, as well as accepting the fate of living under the shadow of a complex scheme.

Wong's clanspeople had to be mindful of their status because it was ambivalent and precarious. The race- and class-based Chinese Exclusion Act of 1882 and subsequent legislation proscribed the entry of Chinese into the United States, except for the exempt classes (merchants, teachers, students, diplomats, and visitors). Such laws were the outcomes of long-held prejudices against "Orientals," rabid nativism in the 1870s that was grounded in labor competition, and the jostling for power in state and national politics. These laws were not repealed until 1943. Even then, for years afterward, a tiny yearly quota of 105 kept many Chinese away, although much larger numbers of persons entered legally as brides or other family members of U.S. citizens.

To qualify for admission, most prospective Chinese immigrants found themselves in a dilemma: either they become complicit in a scheme to violate U.S. immigration law or they abandon any hope of legally landing in the country. Over time, at least thirty thousand Chinese, and probably many more than that, chose the former.[14] The paper son scheme involved a complex network of overlapping family, clan, friendship, and even business ties that stretched across the Pacific Ocean. Clanspeople who resided in the United States offered "slots" (it was almost always "sons" that they claimed to U.S. authorities) for entry as well as jobs or business opportunities—as demonstrated both in Wong's and Jee See Wing's (Wong's real father) cases. Kinfolk in their Chinese villages offered information, money, and coaching so that potential immigrants could succeed in their duplicity.[15] Wong clearly was a recipient of such assistance; in return, his father promised to aid the immigration of the son of Wong's paper father, who was a distant cousin.

The scheme Wong and his relatives participated in was not flawless. United States immigration authorities, well aware of the duplicity, were relentless in their efforts to ferret out the "paper sons." How they carried out these efforts exhibited deeply entrenched institutionalized racism reflected in their attitudes toward the Chinese, the system established to process such new arrivals, and the treatment of those detained for interrogations. New immigrants also encountered other pressures: the officials "mistrusted the entire register of documentary evidence" even as they imposed an "upward spiral of evidentiary requirements upon Chinese immigrants."[16]

Although Wong and See Wing succeeded in passing the immigration-clearance process, at least one of See Wing's paper brothers was denied entry and forced to return to China.[17] With the threat of deportation heavy on their minds, new arrivals suffered the emotional pressure of having to discard their real identities and assume new ones. Detained in a confined space in the sparsely furnished and often overcrowded wooden barracks of the Angel Island Immigration Station (established in 1910 and closed down in 1940) and facing the gauntlet of repeated interrogations, only the most self-assured individuals overcame these odds.[18]

Even after Wong cleared the hurdle, the legacy of the "paper son" scheme continued to haunt his life and that of his family. After the war, See Wing, Wong's father, discovered just how fragile his paper identity was. When he made an error in a document and used "Gee" instead of "Jee" as stated in his immigration records, that error caught up with him and delayed his return to the United States.

Yee Kim Suey, the "war bride" Wong brought with him from China in 1947, was subjected to scrutiny by U.S. officials who were, in spite of the repeal of the Chinese Exclusion Act in 1943, still highly doubtful of the true identities of these Chinese war brides. Wong's coaching of Yee for the interrogation, so as to avoid the fate of a long detention, was repeated by countless of other nervous Chinese GIs and separated, anxious Chinese husbands.[19] Like other Chinese war brides, to protect an entire complex immigration network, Yee had to conceal her husband's true past and provide information that matched his fictive ties. Wong's retelling of this part of their marriage is highly emotional, reflective, and deeply personal—no other published autobiography has covered this theme in such detail. This part of the autobiography should also remind readers of the significance of the war bride migration. Not only did this migration lead to the establishment of new Chinese nuclear families in the United States, but in other instances it also reunited families long separated by gender-biased exclusion laws. The days of the so-called bachelors' society had come to an end; Chinese immigrants were now making the transition from sojourners to settlers.[20]

The fraudulent scheme eventually caught up with the Wongs. In 1956 the Immigration and Naturalization Service (INS) initiated the Confession Program, which allowed Chinese immigrants to correct their contorted family history by confessing their illegal entry. This program had a sinister quality: Cold War fears of communist infiltration into the United States by way of the paper son scheme had prompted it. Even before the program was initiated, leftist Chinese Americans had been picked up and subjected to intense interrogation, and a small number were deported. INS agents raided Chinese business establishments and searched residences. The witchhunt evoked a general panic in Chinatowns, discouraging Chinese from confessing.[21] The Wongs would never have confessed had their paper relative not done likewise, thus implicating his real and paper families, including the Wongs. Wong's candor in revealing this part of his life enables the reader to understand the "cost" of this Confession Program.

Wong's autobiography is also significant in another important way: it remains one of the few published works that offers insight into Chinese American adolescent life in the interwar years. Furthermore, though existing published autobiographies that advance such an understanding were written by the second-generation and native-born, Wong's is probably the first by an immigrant. What is perhaps most significant of all is that this is the first one situated in the Midwest, a region that uniquely shaped Wong's acculturation along a different trajectory than that of other Chinese Americans.

Second-generation Chinese Americans who resided in heavily populated Asian communities of the West Coast came under the influence of their peers, ethnic communities, schooling, churches, and mainstream popular culture. Their opportunities for acculturation were varied and took place in various settings. Wong's only contact with the non-Chinese world was through his teachers, and even less, through his peers. Work at the family-owned restaurant kept him away from those influences enjoyed by coethnics on the West Coast.[22] Because he lived in a region with a minuscule Asian population, he escaped the influences of Americanized coethnics. Similarly to most Asian American children before World War II, his labor was tied to the family economy.

Unlike Euro-American children, Asian children of working-class and petit bourgeois backgrounds fell outside the sheltered childhood ideal. The preoccupation of Euro-American children with play and schooling and their dependency on elders were foreign to Asian children's upbringing.[23] In the interwar years Asian children in the countryside toiled as farmhands, fruit pickers, cannery workers, and store helpers. Children were also drawn into housework and child care, a trend that continued into the postwar years, as witnessed in the Wong household. In urban centers, children such as those in St. Louis's Hop Alley, the local Chinatown, labored before and after school in family-owned enterprises ranging from laundries to grocery stores.[24]

Such labor, whether in urban centers or the countryside, took place against a backdrop of labor segmentation and racial segregation. Wong's recollections of life in Wichita (as opposed to his life in the army or elsewhere in the United States), however, suggest that he suffered little *blatant* racial discrimination. One exception took place in the years following World War II with respect to whites' fears of "block busting," or the enforcement of housing segregation. Other instances of racial conflict involved his offspring: daughter Wilma, who claimed being a victim of job discrimination when she tried to find a teaching job, and son David, who endured name calling during the height of the Vietnam War.

One reason for Wong's low exposure to racism revolved around the minuscule Chinese (and Asian) population in Kansas until recent times. In 1930, census takers enumerated 53 Chinese men and 7 Chinese women in the state of Kansas. This total of 60 climbed to 133 in 1940, which broke down as 124 men and 9 women. Yet the total number each year made up only 0.01 percent of the state's total population. Even though the total Chinese population in the state after World War II continued to grow—from 315 in 1950 to 537 ten years later—as a percentage of the state's population, it inched upward by only 0.01 percent.[25]

The "invisibility" of the Chinese population in Wichita undercut any perception that it represented an economic or social threat to white society. Chinese American residential and occupational concentration confined to the parameters of several blocks in the downtown business and commercial district also meant that the Chinese experienced limited contact with a broad spectrum of other Americans. More important, work in an entirely coethnic setting—specifically in the kitchen—that did not bring them in contact with white customers consumed all of their time, leaving them with little opportunity to interact with whites in churches, parks, theaters, or other public spaces. Furthermore, because Chinese in Wichita depended on coethnics for employment—almost wholly in the Chinese American restaurant business that non-Chinese did not participate in—white hysteria over "Oriental" competition for jobs, which ran rampant in California, was preempted.[26] Finally, unlike late-nineteenth-century immigrants caught up in the heights of the exclusionary movement, Wong came to a prewar United States where heated anti-Chinese sentiments had cooled off to some degree.

Though *blatant* racial discrimination did not completely suffuse Wong's adolescence and his later post–World War II adult life in Wichita, the few relationships he had with white Americans fell largely within the parameters of a paternalistic superior-subordinate relationship. His teachers and fellow students were helpful, but Wong never formed close relationships with any of them. Wong was grateful for their benevolence, but that did not mean these were his intimate friends. Wong recounts other individuals who had extended their magnanimity: the boarding house lady and a minister in Kansas City, the immigration official onboard the ship that brought him and his bride back to the United States, and business customers who shared their resources with him. Yet they too lived on the margins of Wong's social life. Still, Wong was overly grateful for their benevolence, so much so that readers would be reminded of the ingratiating reactions of another Asian immigrant, Mary Paik Lee, as documented in her autobiography, *Quiet Odyssey*. (See the appendix for a longer discussion of the commonalities between Wong's and Lee's works.)

Wong's life could typify that of many other Asian Americans who lived and worked in this region during the exclusion era. First, the immigration of Wong's kinfolk to the Midwest mirrored that of other Chinese immigrants who either fled or avoided the exclusion era's anti-Chinese prejudice and declining economic opportunity on the West Coast.[27] Later waves of immigrants like Wong himself came directly from China to the Midwest, drawn by existing kinship ties in the heartland or by news of economic opportunities, or both. This pattern of migration suggests that Chinese Americans have not necessarily radiated from the West Coast, as the Asian American history's master narrative, with its broadly paradigmatic West Coast emphasis, would have us believe.[28] By 1920, two years before Wong's biological father immigrated to the United States, only about 63 percent of the Chinese populace lived in the American West; the rest had scattered all over the Midwest, South, and East Coast. Ten years later, in 1930 (about five years before Wong himself immigrated), the U.S. Census estimated that that figure had dropped a little to 59.8 percent; the gradual dispersal continued to play out.[29]

Yet there were few Chinese in the Midwest throughout the first four decades of the twentieth century. In 1900 the size of the Chinese population in the following states was as follows: Ohio, 371; Indiana, 207; Illinois, 1,503; Michigan, 240; Wisconsin, 212; Minnesota, 166; Iowa, 104; Missouri, 449; Nebraska, 180; and Kansas, 39. Thirty years later the numbers had increased for all states: Ohio, 1,425; Indiana, 279; Illinois, 3,192; Michigan, 1,081; Wisconsin, 363; Minnesota, 524; Iowa, 153; Missouri, 634; Nebraska, 194; and Kansas, 60. As a percentage of the entire states' populations, Chinese residents still constituted a numerically insignificant presence. In 1900 the percentage of Chinese residents (measured against the total population) in all of the aforesaid midwestern states was around 0.01 percent except for Nebraska's, which was 0.02 percent. Thirty years later, the only state that showed an obvious increase was Illinois (0.04 percent). The percentage inched slightly upward to 0.02 for four states: Ohio, Michigan, Minnesota, and Missouri. The percentage for Indiana, Wisconsin, and Iowa remained the same, while that of Nebraska dropped to 0.01 percent. Little changed a decade later; Chinese residents as a percentage of the total population for these states in 1940 ranged between 0.01 and 0.02 percent.[30]

In the absence of a visible ethnic community, and bereft of "normal" family life, midwestern Asians faced the contradiction of being invisible in the eyes of the larger society and yet remained "different" enough (because their racial marker drew attention in white-dominated areas) to be targets of Americanization, as was the case with Wong's experience with schooling and Christianity. Furthermore, Asian immigrants and their descendants in the Midwest (as well as those in the East and South) were more so the "foreigners within," to borrow Lisa Lowe's phrase, than their coethnics in the "multicultural" Pacific Coast. Racial formation in the Midwest, as in the South, was rigidly structured by the dominant black/white model, and as such, Asian Americans found themselves treated by the state and the dominant society as either "white" or "black."[31]

Such policies and actions were often quite arbitrary. For example, Chinese Americans in Louisiana were in 1860 classified as whites, but a decade later they were classified as Chinese, while their biracial children in 1890 could be classified as either blacks or whites.[32] The midwestern states of Nebraska and Missouri classified a person as "black" if he or she met the minimal requirement of one-eighth African descent, but states in the Deep South often were more rigid, relying on the so-called one-drop blood rule.

Asians in the Midwest experienced discrimination in distinctive ways. All but two of the anti-Chinese riots—which numbered more than one hundred between the 1850s and 1908—in the nineteenth century took place in the Far West. The one in the Midwest occurred in Milwaukee, Wisconsin, and the southern one in Waynesboro, Georgia. The Milwaukee riot illustrates how societal policing of the boundaries of whiteness demonized Asians as lustful creatures in a way that reminds one of the prevailing southern stereotypes of African Americans. In 1889 an anti-Chinese riot broke out in that city over the arrest of two middle-aged Chinese men charged with taking sexual liberties with underage white girls. Victor Jew, in his study of this racial conflict, suggests that the white mob mentality was no different than lynch disciplining in the post-Reconstruction South. He also argues that unlike anti-Chinese violence in the Far West that was often prompted by labor competition, such a phenomenon in the Midwest was possibly instigated more by overlapping social anxieties about race, gender, and sexuality.[33]

Social anxieties also galvanized an 1886 economic boycott of the twelve Chinese laundries in Wichita. Although they were instigated by the labor organization Order of the Knights of Labor, Julie Courtwright explains that labor competition did not play a role here; rather, the inflammatory, nativistic rhetoric of local newspapers, coupled with the derogatory image of the Chinese during the height of the exclusion era, fueled the boycott.[34] After 1900 little of this earlier racial animosity lingered in Wichita; I know of no evidence of mob violence against Asians elsewhere in the region in the first half of the twentieth century. If race relations in the Midwest were historically shaped far more by social anxieties than by outright economic competition, then racial animosity probably played out in subtle ways, such as social segregation and a segmented labor market, which Wong experienced, rather than as violent hostile encounters.[35] Because racial discrimination against Wong was reportedly indirect, subtle, or irregular, his recollections of it are overshadowed by remembrances of acceptance and mobility.

After Wong left Wichita for wartime service, much of what he experienced was clearly racially grounded. Even his army uniform did not always convince others, including some Chinese, that he was truly an upstanding American. Wong's wartime experiences heightened his racial awareness even as it offered him the opportunity to prove his claim to U.S. birthright, in spite of his paper son status. Wong's encounter with racial discrimination and his motivation for entering service were in step with those of many other Chinese American servicemen.[36] One might also argue that his paper son status imbued him with a sense of urgency to unequivocally prove his Americanism, one that the paper son scheme cast doubts on.

Wong's tour of duty in China was replete with contradictions. During World War II some 13,311 Chinese Americans—nearly 22 percent of adult Chinese males in the United States—were drafted into the armed services. An unknown number—perhaps several thousand, including Wong—volunteered for military service.[37] During World War II most of the Chinese Americans served in integrated units with white soldiers, but approximately 1,200 were in ten all–Chinese American units that were stationed in the China-Burma-India (CBI) theater. Nine of them belonged to the Fourteenth Air Service Group (14th ASG) that operated as part of the Fourteenth Air Force, which also took on the popular name "Flying Tigers."[38] The remaining tenth unit was Wong's, but his—the 987th Signal Company—was the only one that was not an army air corps unit. Wong and his Chinese peers were shunted into segregated units. Furthermore, and more significantly, each of the other nine units had at least a few Euro-American officers; Wong's was the only one wholly made up of Chinese recruits, from privates all the way up to the company commander.

The official reasons for the formation of such segregated units, as pointed out by K. Scott Wong, remain unclear because documents are still unavailable, and much of the following explanation comes from unproven assertions of Chinese American GIs. Chiang Kai-shek, the leader of the Nationalist Chinese government, supposedly made a request to the U.S. government to supply Chinese-speaking soldiers who could provide assistance to both American and Chinese Nationalist forces. Furthermore, as speakers of Chinese, they could facilitate better relations with the local population. However, as it turned out, the U.S. Army, as suggested in Wong's writings, was culturally ignorant of China's diversity of dialects, which the Chinese American servicemen did not necessarily speak. A related explanation for the formation of these all–Chinese American units was that Chiang banked on them to provide the motivation for Chinese in America to funnel monetary support for China's war against Japanese aggression. Finally, because the army retained segregated units well into the Korean War, organizing a large number of drafted Chinese Americans in similar units seemed in step with the armed services' overall organization.[39] These segregated Chinese American units paralleled those established for Japanese Americans during World War II, the most well-known being the highly decorated 442nd Regimental Combat Team.

In the army, Wong and his peers were caught between the black-white dyad of race relations. In the United States, in the perception of white Americans, "Americans" were invariably white and racial minorities black. Chinese (as well as other Asian) Americans who were clearly not black or white were neither American nor minority.[40] In the United States, Chinese servicemen were positioned uncomfortably in a "gray" area. Wong was given "preferential" treatment by one white quartermaster, slighting an African American officer of a higher rank. In several instances, however, Wong and his comrades found themselves the victims of racial hysteria during the war years.[41] Unconvinced that American soldiers could be anything but white, some Euro-Americans exhibited color prejudice toward them. Wong offers no observations of the relationship between white American soldiers and local Chinese in China. Anecdotal accounts by other Chinese American servicemen, however, suggest that white soldiers were often impatient and contemptuous of the local Chinese; such incidents must have also raised the racial consciousness of Chinese American GIs.[42]

In China the tables were somewhat turned. Most of Wong's fellow Chinese American soldiers considered themselves "Americans" even if that identity was questioned in the United States, and some of them were now serving in the land of their birth. Garbed in the GI uniform, Wong and his compatriots were readily identifiable as part of the American military forces. Though warmly treated as allies of the

Chinese Nationalist forces who came to China's aid against Japanese aggression—an observation Wong writes about—Chinese American servicemen keenly felt a divide between themselves and their Chinese peers, and the local population. Accustomed to modern conveniences and a higher standard of living, they were typically taken aback by the level of destitution they found in China.[43]

As a recent immigrant who was born and partly raised in China, and who had also been exposed to Chinese city life, Wong exhibited more sympathy toward the people he encountered in China than did U.S.-born Chinese Americans, whose recollections make up the bulk of the few scholarly studies on these servicemen. Yet his observations of the conditions faced by Chinese Nationalist troops and the common people reveal just as much of himself: he understood the patent difference in the living standards between the United States and China. In an era of machines and progress China was obviously some distance from modernity—a conclusion also suggested in the recollections of other Chinese American servicemen.[44] Consequently, Chinese American servicemen like Wong most likely became increasingly aware of the definition of their citizenry or American identity, one that did not necessarily entail adherence to or rejection of any given racial-ethnic culture.

Conversely, like other Chinese servicemen, Wong found his ethnic identity also reinforced during his time in the army. If food is a marker of ethnic identity, then the constant references to Chinese food, as well as the desire to seek such food both in China and America, suggests an attempt to maintain an ethnic identity that could set him apart from other American servicemen.[45]

Besides the themes of the paper son scheme and World War II military service, Wong's autobiography also sheds light on the Chinese American family of the postwar years—an underexamined theme in Chinese American history.[46] In so doing, it also offers insights into gender and family roles. Wong writes about the difficulties of raising a family in Wichita, as well as the hardships they suffered. Bereft of the typical family-support network that they would have enjoyed in China, Wong and Yee Kim Suey, his war bride, were left to their own devices.

Even though they fell into the traditional pattern of existing gender hierarchy—he at work, she at home—Yee eventually became restive enough to seek paid labor. She was forced to overcome the language barrier and adapt to hard, physical labor. Yee's experiences echoed to some degree those of other war brides, who also found themselves immersed in a double burden of work in and outside the home, while dealing with a meager household income. Unlike Yee, who did not venture into the labor market until her children had grown up, a number of the war brides were forced to lend a hand in family-run businesses while raising their children.

With their earlier overblown expectations of a good life in America shattered, and then feeling fed up with the endless grind, some women abandoned their husbands, returned to China, and in a few cases even committed suicide.[47] Yee's experiences overall were more positive. Perhaps her husband played a part in determining that outcome. Wong comes across as an even-tempered spouse who took the trouble to teach her the American way of life, from speaking English to cooking. They also seemed to collaborate well in the restaurants, although a thoroughly egalitarian division of labor never emerged in their married life.

Wong in his memoirs also provides a few glimpses into the formative bicultural identity of his children, who belong to the second generation. In the Wong household, the children grew up in an era—1940s through 1960s—when American society underwent cataclysmic change. As the civil rights movement reached a crescendo in the mid-1960s, new legislation and judicial decisions outlawed housing and educational segregation. Institutionalized racism took a heavy hit.

But long-held prejudicial attitudes took a longer time to unravel. The Wong children lived in a racially mixed neighborhood, attended integrated schools, grew up exposed to American popular culture, but socialized primarily with other Chinese youngsters. In the late 1960s Wilma Wong, the younger daughter, encountered job discrimination, while her youngest brother, Edward, became a victim of racial lumping.

The Wong elders counseled the route of accommodation for their children. The parents, attuned to the existing color line in American society, forswore interracial marriage, which their children ultimately abided by. They instilled in their children the need to succeed in education so as to overcome racial barriers and open the doors of economic opportunity. The American-born Wong children, for their part, aspired to be American, accommodated being Chinese, and offered minimal resistance to their circumstances. In some respects they were no different than their Chinese American peers who grew up in that Cold War era of conformity—all of them felt the pressure to be more "American" than "Chinese," even though in reality they were bicultural.[48]

Perhaps the parents' keen interest in maintaining transnational ties to the homeland played a part in fostering the children's Chinese-ness. As detailed in the book's final two chapters, even though Wong had established a family in the United States, he kept in close contact with his relatives in China. The remittance for his mother and brother to immigrate to the United States, the monetary contribution for the family's memorial building, and the periodic visits to China attest to his transnational linkages to his birthplace; so do Yee's efforts to sponsor family members to immigrate to the United States. His children's Chinese-ness is probably complicated; like other U.S.-born Chinese Americans, they have visited China several times. In so doing, Wong's children participated in "cultural tourism," enabling them to reroot themselves in the ancestral homeland and explore a new Chinese American identity embracing both transnational and nation-state-bound ties.[49]

American Paper Son examines a number of forces that shaped Chinese American life during the twentieth century: immigration laws and resistance to them; split households and family reunification; acculturation; labor and ethnic entrepreneurship; wartime service; ethnic identity; transnationalism; and gender and generational dynamics. While these topics are of interest to scholars, general readers will find much with which they can identify. Wong's memoirs reflect the universal human themes of adaptation to change and the will to persevere. It also gives voice to the countless isolated Chinese immigrants who made the American Midwest their home but who lived in the shadow of exclusion, and it does this with grace, wry humor, and keen observations.

CHAPTER 1

❦ ❦ ❦   Coming to America

My birth name is Mar Ying Wing, but my naturalized name is Wayne Hung Wong. My paper birth date is August 9, 1922, and my paper name is Wong Hung Yin. I was born in Changlong village, Baisha district, Taishan County, Guangdong Province, in southern China.

Our farming village was about thirty to forty miles from the South China Sea coast. Like all other neighboring villages the houses in ours were laid out in a gridlike pattern. Between narrow lanes, houses were densely packed and ran in straight rows from the front of the village to the back. Beyond this cluster of dwellings irregularly laid-out fields and low hills dotted the undulating landscape.

Life was slow in that village, but always productive. It was never languid. Crops, particularly rice, grew throughout the year. The soil was fertile and the weather mild year-round. Occasionally rain fell in torrents, and then quickly the sun emerged again.[1] I had never seen snow in the winter until I came to the United States.

I would like to begin my convoluted story by recounting my family's genealogy. To the Chinese the family tree is important: it enables future generations to know of their roots, to learn where they came from. To know the past is to appreciate the ancestors, and to accept the idea that one must always be a good citizen and never bring disgrace to the family. A Chinese man's understanding of the family genealogy is just as important as his practice of ancestor worship—they both reinforce one's ties to extended family of the past and present.

My ancestors came a long time ago to southern China from the north. The original ancestors lived in the Yellow River valley. About eight hundred years ago the Mars immigrated to Guangdong. Four hundred years later the family moved farther inland to Taishan.[2] My great-great-grandfather, Cheng Foo, was part of the twenty-second generation of Mars.

In Changlong village my great-grandfather, Mar Oy Shee, was a well-to-do and thrifty farmer who owned many parcels of bounteous land. He even leased some of them out to tenant farmers to plant rice, and they in turn paid him a percentage of their harvest. Oy Shee also hired a number of field hands to tend his crops, which besides rice included taro, melons, and water chestnuts.[3] These crops were then sold in nearby market towns in exchange for cash. The field hands also tended to chickens, geese, and pigs and produced preserved foods such as salted vegetables, fish, and shrimp. Oy Shee had everything he needed to provide for his family.

Oy Shee had a large family—four sons and one daughter. In the Chinese tradition it is the father's duty to have his dutiful children married off at a young age. Oy Shee provided a house for each of the sons to serve as a home. The daughter, however, received a generous dowry to start her own family. His numbers two, three, and four sons eventually left their families in China in the very late nineteenth century and went to Penang, Malaya (now Malaysia), to earn a livelihood.[4] They became entrepreneurs in the textile industry.

I have never seen my great-grandfather, but I still vividly remember my great-grandmother, whose family name was Cheng, but her maiden name I never knew. I remember her sitting in an easy padded chair. She was a petite woman with small feet. Her feet, a mere two or three inches long, were in fact bound, forcing her to totter rather than walk like other people. As a young boy I never understood why she put herself through such "torture."[5] Great-grandmother certainly never "wandered" afar. Great-grandmother lived a long life—she was ninety-three when she passed away, and I was about four or five years old at that time.

I am not sure when my great-grandfather died, but in 1906 my grandfather and his three brothers pooled their resources and built a large house as a memorial to him. It was a two-story brick building that mixed traditional Chinese and Western motifs. Ornate Chinese carvings embellished the roofline and window frames, while a simple portico without columns fronted an iron gate that served as the main door. The windows that flanked the gate were long and arched at the top. Above the windows traditional Chinese landscape art graced the marble slabs. On the second floor a balcony decorated with flowerlike carvings hung over the portico. Later a Chinese lady schoolteacher used this memorial house to open an all-girls school. My mother, Wong Sen Kew, who never bound her feet, was one of her students for many years.[6]

My grandfather, Mar Bong Shui, was the number one son. Garbed in his long, flowing Chinese silk robe that only the well-heeled could afford, and possessing a serious demeanor, he looked aloof, even haughty. A fairly well-educated man, he operated an import and export company called South-North Herbal Company in Hong Kong. He also owned real estate properties. His trading ties were extensive; they stretched well across the Pacific Ocean. Years before I was born, Bong Shui's business was booming. Like his father he was a shrewd businessman. Later on his economic success facilitated the emigration of his offspring.[7]

In his family life, however, Bong Shui met dire misfortune. His first wife, Yee See, gave birth to five daughters, one after another. The Gods seemed to have cast an evil spell on him. Bong Shui was very disappointed after the birth of his fifth daughter; daughters did not count in traditional Chinese families. After all, one day they would belong to another family, once they were married off. The Chinese proverb "A boy is born facing in; a girl is born facing out" explains the girls' status. Sons also supported their parents in their old age, and after their deaths performed the necessary ancestral rites. Bong Shui also truly wanted a son to continue the family lineage. So did his first wife.[8]

With Yee See's consent, Bong Shui decided to take another woman to be his second wife, one whom he had met in Hong Kong. The second wife—Soo See, my natal grandmother—was taller yet stockier, even more masculine looking than the first wife, but unlike the latter had no bound feet. His second wife brought him good fortune. The following year his first wife gave birth to a boy in the early part of the year. His second wife gave birth to a second son—my father—in October of the same year. Bong Shui now had two sons in one year. The following year his second wife had a miscarriage. It was determined to be a girl. The second wife was saddened by the loss. The next year his second wife gave birth to his third son. A year or so later his first wife gave birth to his fourth son. Within four years Bong Shui gained four sons; he secured the assurance that the family name and heritage would now pass on to the subsequent generations.

With an expanding family grandfather built two large brick houses, one for numbers one and four sons and their families and another one for the number two and number three sons and their families. Later on my father renovated one of these two houses. The renovated house then had two stories. The first floor featured an oversized kitchen and across from the main door the revered family altar. There were two bedrooms on this floor. The other floor, with wooden railings, opened onto the first floor, creating a traditional Chinese courtyard ambiance.

My grandfather's three sons—numbers one, two, and four—as well as his number four daughter, eventually immigrated to *Gum Saan* (Cantonese for "Gold Mountain," which refers to the United States)[9] to make their livings. Unlike many Chinese immigrants, all of them had married in China and raised families there before emigrating. The three brothers were all eventually buried in the Wichita Park Cemetery. My grandfather's number three son stayed in China and Hong Kong to look after his father's manifold business interests and to carry on the family tradition. At this writing he is still alive and living in the house grandfather built for him. He turned 101 years of age in November 2003.

Grandfather's number four daughter, Mar Yell Sen, married Wong Gin Wing in 1921. Gin Wing was a businessman, and consequently he was able to bring his wife to the United States. Though he was not a citizen, the laws allowed him to raise a family in this new land.[10] In those days it was a rarity. The number of Chinese men who immigrated to the United States vastly outnumbered the women. The sex ratio was something akin to 600 men to 1 woman.[11] Gin Wing and Yell Sen ran a restaurant in Evanston, Wyoming, and raised two boys and four girls. Their children are all very prosperous today.

In later years Uncle Gin Wing told me that my father, Mar Tung Jing, the number two son, left China for the United States three months after I was born in 1922.[12] Gin Wing and Yell Sen both left China for the United States soon after my father left the ancestral land. All of them left the country to find better economic opportunities abroad. By the early 1920s China was in turmoil and there was much chaos. Decades of wars, floods, famines, and droughts had worn many Taishanese down. My grandfather was more fortunate than other clanspeople, but the destitution in the countryside led him to think ahead to the future.[13]

Because my grandfather was an exporter and importer—and thus was a merchant—the best way for him to get my father to *Gum Saan* would be for him to pass as a bill collector.[14] So Grandfather—and luckily he had the means—had to buy another bill collector's legal paper in order for him to come to the United States. Father's paper name was Jee See Wing. He stayed and worked in San Francisco—probably toiling as a restaurant worker or manual laborer—until the spring of 1924.[15]

His third cousin, Henry Mar, and my father's classmate in China, King Mar, soon wrote and urged him to come to Wichita, Kansas, to join them in a restaurant partnership that served American and Chinese foods.[16] He accepted their offer because he knew that by owning a business he had steady employment, whereas if he had continued as an employee, his future was uncertain and he would have earned far less.[17] After all, most *gam saan haak* (Cantonese for "Gold Mountain guests") as wage laborers found only *hek fu* (Cantonese for "taking in pain" or "adversity").[18] Not only did most of them remain in poverty and suffer the brunt of racism, but their low socioeconomic status prevented them from reuniting with their families in China as well. I assume Father wished to avoid that tragic fate.

I think it was around 1900 when many oil fields were discovered around El Dorado and Wichita.[19] Originally opened in 1917, my father's restaurant offered twenty-four-hour service to accommodate these oil-field workers and cattlemen.[20] The original owners of the restaurant had made their fortunes and were advanced in age. They were old-time sojourners who wished to return to China to spend their golden years in retirement. They wanted to reunite with their families, who had lived apart from them for decades.[21] It was an excellent opportunity for my father to buy into an established enterprise.

The restaurant was called the "Pan-American Café." There were altogether six business partners, all of them surnamed Mar, and my talented father became the cook for Chinese dishes.[22] The restaurant was open seven days a week and was Wichita's first Chinese-owned restaurant to be air-conditioned. As late as the late 1930s, the Pan-American remained the only such restaurant in the city to offer this modern comfort.

The Pan-American served both American and Chinese food. About 70 percent of the menu was American food and the other 30 was Chinese. Chinese entrées included chow mein, chop suey, lo mein, and egg foo yung. On the American side, customers could order roast beef, pork chops, steaks, fried catfish, meatloaf, beef stew, fried chicken, roast chicken, beef liver and onions, and grilled salmon. The business thrived and reaped profits for the owners.

Between 1920 and 1941, based on what I learned from my father, there were ten other establishments owned by Chinese immigrants in Wichita similar to the Pan-American Café.[23] Nearly all of the restaurants were clustered within a four-block area bounded by William, First, Broadway, and Market Streets.[24] Many of these restaurants were owned by a succession of owners. When the original owners left to return to China for good, the business would change hands. The Great Depression also took a toll on a number of these restaurants; some simply went bust.[25]

During World War II the three aircraft companies in Wichita—Beech Aircraft, Cessna Aircraft, and Boeing Aircraft—were running twenty-four hours a day, seven days a week. The Wichita population more than doubled because of the upsurge in national defense work.[26] There were two other Chinese restaurants at that time: the Holly Café at 119 West Douglas and the Fairland Café at 116 South Broadway. The Holly was just a block from the Broadview Hotel on Douglas and Waco Streets, and so guests of the hotel often became its customers. Similarly the Fairland was a mere half block from the fifteen-story Allis Hotel on William and South Broadway Streets, and also enjoyed the patronage of the hotel guests. Father's restaurant was just across from the popular Lassen Hotel; a cabaret in the hotel led many to the Pan-American, which served numerous meals to happy revelers. These restaurants and the ones that preceded them were located in the downtown district at a time when people still shopped there. Both the Holly and Fairland were also open seven days a week and twenty-four hours a day. Like the Pan-American Café, they too benefited from the wartime boom and its concomitant demand for services.[27] After the war, the national defense work in Wichita came to an end. The economy was slowing down.[28] Beginning in the 1950s suburbs mushroomed and city dwellers moved away from the downtown district. New businesses joined the migration and established themselves in the suburbs, where plenty of free parking was available. The downtown district entered into a long decline as stores closed and streets emptied of automobiles and pedestrians.

The younger (my) Chinese generation were the World War II veterans who earned the right to bring their wives as war brides to the United States. The men wanted to start their families and their own businesses, or pursue other professions. They were unwilling to support the existing family-owned enterprises. Consequently there was no one to take over the old restaurant, and the Pan-American Café closed in 1969.[29]

During the interwar years the relative success of the restaurant enabled my father to make three trips to China. Subsequently I had two brothers and one sister. On his first trip in 1928 I was six years old. I remember that he took the family to Hong Kong to visit Grandfather, and to Guangzhou, where my mother's older brother practiced as a Western medical doctor, having earned his medical degree in France. On this trip my father bought a three-story building in Guangzhou to supplement the family income. The following year a brother joined the family.[30]

Every time he came to China he regaled us with stories of how easy it was to make one's fortunes in Gold Mountain. Dressed in his western suit and hat, he returned each time with a trunkful of clothing, toiletries, gold coins, and jewelry. He convinced us that life in the United States was good.

During the years when my father lived in the United States, my mother did not live with his parents in China. Our family house was in the same village as my grandparents', but much smaller. In fact the building, separated from my grandparents' by three alleys, was divided into two units—one part for us, and the other for Uncle Sum Jing's family. Behind us, separated by one vacant lot, was another dwelling also divided into two units—one for Uncle Chee Jing and another for Uncle Sai Jing. None of the sons or their families lived with their parents.[31]

My mother was the daughter of a lumber businessman in Guangzhou and completed the equivalent of elementary school. A demure, petite woman who wore her hair short and often permed, she stood only four feet eleven inches. With large pearl-shaped eyes, high cheekbones, and a high forehead, she looked fragile, like a porcelain dish, and yet she was independent, even strong.

For decades Mother lived apart from Father, while he ventured into the outside world to find his fortune. During that long separation this "grass widow" (a woman living apart from her husband) raised four children and managed the family finances with the $100 remittance she received from Father, which arrived promptly every third month. She must have been lonely at times, relying only on letters from Father for solace.

Living apart from her two mothers-in-law, Mother did not have to tend to their needs. Neither of the mothers-in-law were jealous of her. They were not envious of Mother's status as the wife of a Gold Mountain emigrant; I suppose Grandfather's business success preempted any such feelings. Unlike some other women in the village, Mother never had to till the expansive rice fields or work outside the home; the money Father regularly sent home was sufficient to live on. Mother also had at her disposal the help of a young servant who took care of the endless chores of cooking and housekeeping.[32]

Wootip ("Butterfly"), my mother's village, was about two and a half miles from our village. Whenever Mother went to visit her mother, Grandma, and this was quite often, she took me with her. Along the way I recall meeting gossipy female relatives who bantered endlessly with my mother about the stories they had heard of Gold Mountain men who kept concubines in America, or those who led dissolute lives abroad. In those days villagers fiercely competed to build better homes using remittances from abroad, and that stoked such pettiness. If Mother did react to those tales designed purposefully to insinuate that her husband had abandoned her, she never showed it in public. She kept her composure. Mother was, however, mindful of any gossip that she might be a nonvirtuous woman; she never spent the night away at Grandma's house and never ventured far from the villages surrounding ours.[33]

Whenever we visited Grandma she always had something for me to eat, usually fruits or nuts. Unlike my paternal great-grandmother, Grandma did not bind her feet. She had to work both inside and outside the home. Even though she was the wife of a merchant she did her share of raising the poultry, tending to the vegetable garden, sewing and repairing clothes, and overseeing the preparation of daily meals. Later Grandma moved to Guangzhou to be with Dr. Wong's family and her daughter; as she grew older, a widowed Grandma longed for family life.

I recall an unfortunate childhood incident. I think I was nine years old. I was playing "tag" with another young boy in a large tree with many branches. About two hours before, a heavy downpour drenched the tree limbs, leaving leaves glistening from unevaporated drops of water. This boy was furiously chasing me. So I leapt faster from one branch to another. The distance between us was disappearing. At one point I leapt and the heel of my right foot landed on a limb, but I slipped. I went tumbling downward fourteen feet to the ground, and became unconscious from 4:30 P.M. until 10:00 P.M. One of our farmhands ran to a nearby small town, Baisha, to fetch the medical doctor. Quickly he rode his horse to our house. He examined me and found no broken bones. I only suffered a few minor bruises. I was indeed a lucky boy. My mother, however, made a big fuss over it; she was most protective of me, her eldest son.

My grandfather came back to the village to visit the family about three times a year. He always brought gifts, impressing us with his generosity. Every time he came to visit he would invite me to dinner, and then he would take me to town for a special treat of chocolate-covered candies. In the summer, Mother took me and my brother to visit Dr. Wong in Guangzhou and to Hong Kong to visit Grandfather. My grandfather passed away when I was about ten. He was only sixty-four.

My father made his second trip to China in 1934. I gained a sister in 1935, and in that year he returned to the United States. By then it was time for me to emigrate.

The U.S. Congress passed the Chinese Exclusion Act on May 6, 1882, as well as other supplementary laws, long before I was born.[34] These were in effect discriminatory acts against the Chinese. The Chinese were singled out solely because of their skin color. No Chinese were permitted to work for the State of California. In some locales Chinese attended segregated schools, and in others they were run out of town.[35] The smoldering coals of hostility burst into flames; the Chinese were rounded up like swine and routed out of the cities and towns.[36] The laws barred Chinese men from bringing their wives and families to the United States.[37]

The blatantly racist immigration laws did not completely choke off Chinese immigration. Chinese immigrants found ingenious ways to enter the country. The Chinese found one way or another to come to the United States for freedom and a better life. The 1882 act, however, forced 90 percent of Chinese immigrants to be liars and frauds.[38] The only way for one to immigrate legally to the United States was to be a son of a U.S. citizen or a native son, but because few could legally claim either status, most were forced to resort to the "paper son" scheme. I was one of them, and so were a number of my relatives.

My "paper" father's name was Wong Wing Lock. His real name was Mar Moy Jing, and he lived in a village near ours. He and my father were third cousins. Moy Jing had an older brother by the name of Henry Mar. Around 1906 he and his brother entered the United States illegally from Mexico via El Paso, Texas.[39] Having journeyed across the Pacific on an American ship, they entered Mexico by way of a port on the coast of Baja California and somehow made their way to El Paso.

It was fortuitous for them that the San Francisco earthquake happened in 1906. This was a large stroke of fortune for all Chinese. The Gods smiled on them. The earthquake destroyed the county courthouse, while the rapidly moving fire burned all of the birth certificate records. Any Chinese person who could bring two witnesses (Chinese witnesses were acceptable) to verify that they were native born were issued a birth certificate attesting to their native-born status.[40] Taking advantage of the turn of events, Henry Mar found two witnesses to verify that he was a native born of the name Mar Jill Jing. Similarly,

Moy Jing persuaded two witnesses to verify that he was Wong Wing Lock, a native born in the United States.[41]

With their birth certificates in hand they returned to China in 1910 to get married and raise families.[42] Henry Mar brought his two sons to Wichita, Kansas, and thus established his roots in Wichita. He left his two daughters in China. The eldest daughter, however, did immigrate to the United States with her husband in 1964; the youngest never left China.

Moy Jing's number one son was Wong Hung Doon and he was born in 1911.[43] During World War II Hung Doon was drafted in Chicago and then served as a cook in the U.S. Army in the South Pacific theater for almost four years. After the war he changed his name to William D. Marjo. On December 3, 2003, he passed away in a nursing home in El Cerrito, California. My daughters, Linda and Wilma, who lived nearby, visited him often to keep him company. Wing Lock came back to the United States in 1911. He and two of his friends opened a café in Modesto, California.

In 1921 Moy Jing, or Wing Lock, went to China to visit his family for two years. His number two son, Wong Hung Yin, was born in 1922. I was also born in 1922. Moy Jing sailed back to the United States in 1923 with his thirteen-year-old number one son, Hung Doon.[44] At the immigration office in San Francisco he duly reported to the official that his number two son, Wong Hung Yin, was born on August 9, 1922, and that his wife was once again pregnant.

In 1929 Wing Lock, along with his number one son, Hung Doon, returned to China. Just before leaving the United States Wing Lock reminded the immigration official that when he had returned to the country in 1923 he had reported that his wife was pregnant. In 1923 he had indeed gained another son by the name of Wong Hung Que. Eventually Hung Que immigrated to the United States as King Wong; he served in World War II's European theater in the Tank Corps with General Patton's Third Army, and today lives in Portland, Oregon. Number one son, Hung Doon, was married in 1930. Both Wing Lock and Hung Doon—the latter without his wife or child—returned to the United States in 1931.[45] Upon his arrival Wing Lock duly lodged the claim with the immigration authorities that he now had a number four son named Hung On. In truth his new child was a girl, and she never immigrated to the United States.[46] My guess is that Wing Lock planned to later sell this slot to a relative in search of a way to enter the United States. Hung Doon himself reported he had gained a boy named Gin Kin.

Sometime either in 1934 or 1935 Hung Doon returned to China. In the spring of 1935, probably in early April, Hung Doon came to our house. He said to me, "Hong Shook [Uncle, which refers to my father] and my father have made arrangements for us to go to America together in November. Here is the deposition book [about 6" x 9" in dimension] and it contains sixty pages. I want you to study and memorize every detail in this book. From the beginning to the end and from the end to the beginning. Whether or not the immigration services will allow you to enter the United States will depend on how accurate each of our depositions corroborate with each other's testimony. After two weeks we will get together to discuss how we are doing."[47]

The first section of the deposition book dealt with the village. It contained a minutely detailed diagram of the village, showing names of the surrounding villages, the layout of the houses, and the locations of the water well, the outhouse, and the family vegetable garden. The book also described the materials the various structures were made of. The second section was a detailed diagram of the family's house. It showed the layout of the rooms as well as where the tables, chairs, water urn, urine urn, cooking stoves, and other pieces of furniture were placed, along with where each family member slept.

The third section was a detailed diagram listing all family members, with their names and birth dates. All of the relatives and their relationships to each other were outlined—grandparents, parents, brothers, sisters, in-laws, cousins, relatives, and so on. One thing in our favor was that my village and Hung Doon's village were only a half mile apart. All the names in the deposition were as named and known to everyone in the extended family. Hung Doon and I met and talked twice in May.[48]

In June 1935 I had finished my sixth-grade Chinese education in the village. As previously recounted, my mother had a brother who was a physician, and also two younger sisters, all of whom were living in Guangzhou. Mother decided—probably to get closer to her own natal family—to move herself, her children, and a *mui tsai* (young Chinese domestic servant) to live in Guangzhou in the building Father owned. She would live there for a number of years until Father returned to China.[49] Hung Doon and his wife also moved to Guangzhou to reside so that we could continue to meet and discuss the contents of the deposition book.

In 1935 the United States was still in a deep economic depression. Moy Jing wanted to return to China to visit his family and to bring his own son, Hung Yin, to the United States. Deep in debt, Moy Jing ran a restaurant that had fallen on hard times. Clearly he lacked the means to bring his son to the United States.

My father, a more successful restaurateur, had the money to help make it possible. So Moy Jing made a deal with my father that I would come first as Hung Yin. This also fulfilled the promise he made to my father in 1922 that he would have a "paper" for me to immigrate to the United States. That promise apparently was made when both my father and Moy Jing went to a temple in the village to burn incense and pay homage to the Gods for the birth of their respective sons.[50]

My father paid Moy Jing $1,200 for the paper. He also paid Hung Doon $300 for his testimony in support of mine. Father had been saving all this money—which in those days was a large sum—for a long time.[51] Subsequently Moy Jing used the payment he received from my father to return to China in 1936, and in 1937 he came back to the United States with his number two son (Hung Yin), who passed himself off as the number three son, Hung Que.

Before I left for America, or *Mei Kuo* (Cantonese for "Flowery Flag"),[52] I had heard about this golden land. The majority of the people in Taishan had relatives who lived in Hong Kong, Southeast Asia, Australia, Canada, or the United States. For example, my mother's sister married an Overseas Chinese man of the Mar surname and they settled in Seattle, Washington. Many of the buildings in the villages—the elementary school, memorial buildings, and brick houses decorated with Western motifs—were built using the remittances sent by Overseas Chinese. Villagers sometimes depended on remittances from America for their subsistence.[53] My father, during his intermittent visits home, regaled us with tales of American automobiles, tall buildings, and gold ready for the picking off the streets. So I knew that America was *Gum Saan,* or Gold Mountain—the place where fortunes could be made.[54]

Hung Doon and I left Guangzhou—and our families—toward the end of October 1935 for Hong Kong. Because I was the first—and the eldest—child to leave her protective care, Mother wept openly. Grief stricken, she stood alone on the embankment of the river as Hung Doon and I boarded the riverboat that took us to Hong Kong. From the busy port of Hong Kong we boarded the crowded Canadian Empress Liner SS *Princess Alice* to Victoria, British Columbia. Hundreds of Chinese emigrants, as well as a small mixture of Europeans and Americans, were packed into this ship. There was no particular reason why we chose to enter the United States via Canada; we simply followed the route established by the passenger liner.[55]

During our long journey of thirty-three days across the Pacific Ocean I was repeatedly seasick. The rolling waves and constant motion were merciless on my young body. Being holed up in the foul-smelling steerage, the combination of intermingling body odor and the absence of fresh air simply compounded the physical torment suffered by those of us packed into this large room with only our canvas beds as personal space.

Notwithstanding my illness, I did spend much time studying the deposition book. Just before we arrived in America I passed the book back to my "brother"; we had been told that the authorities would search my luggage for contraband or evidence of the deposition book. We assumed that the authorities would pay far less attention to Hung Doon because he had resided in the United States for some years, and had made this trip several times. Later, after the interrogations were over, Hung Doon passed the book back to me and I kept it until I went to war in the 1940s. Somehow between leaving for service and returning to Wichita, the book that I left in the room above the restaurant went missing.[56] In that late fall of 1935, as I traveled across the wide Pacific, I was not afraid for the future; I knew that my father was already here in Wichita, and so our basic needs—making a living, finding a place to sleep, and having food to eat—would be met.

Upon our arrival in Victoria, we took the ferry to Seattle. I think it was about December 1, 1935, when we landed on the Pacific Northwest shores.[57] I was held in this two-story immigration detention building for interrogation and paper processing.[58]

There were about seventy people—all men—in the detention center. Some had been there as long as eighteen months, and some had been there eight or nine. Most would get out in a couple of months.[59] There was not much to do except read newspapers and magazines, write letters, and play games or cards. Still, we were treated well and the food was fairly decent. We slept on wooden beds rather than on canvas cots.

I recall vividly that a group of church missionaries visited us in the last part of December. Looking back, this was my first exposure to Christianity. This visit was probably just before Christmas Day.[60]

The missionaries numbered about twenty. There were three adults, one man and two women, in their late forties. The others were boys and girls about my age, ranging from thirteen to sixteen. There were more girls than boys. They brought gifts such as pens, writing tablets, combs, toothpaste, fruit, cake, and candies. They put on a music program in the day room. There was a piano and about thirty wooden chairs. Some were sitting on the chairs, others standing in the back. They sang some songs in Chinese and others in English; the songs were probably Christmas carols.

I remember this white lady who spoke to me in Cantonese. She asked me my name.

"Wong Hung Yin," I said quietly.

"Do you have an English name?"

"No."

"I would like to give you an English name. How about the name Eddy?"

"Okay," I replied.

When I later attended school in Wichita I decided to go by the name "Wayne," which sounds close to my given Chinese name—I attribute this encounter with the woman missionary for the name change. At that time I knew nothing about Christianity or the celebration of Christmas. I was impressed by their friendliness and their caring, loving attitude. I enjoyed their program and companionship very much.

On December 28 I was called to the interrogation room. I dreaded the process; I knew it was going to be lengthy. The authorities questioned me for two and a half hours.[61] The questions they asked were quite well covered in our deposition book. I supposed that they had already questioned Hung Doon before they questioned me.[62]

During the interrogation they asked me questions about the location of the house, outhouse, school, and other buildings in the village. They hoped to find discrepancies between my testimony and my paper brother's. For example, they asked me to identify the room in which I slept. The officials posed the same question to my paper brother, and if he had placed me in another room then an inconsistency in testimonies would have emerged.

On December 31 they questioned me again for an hour and a half. I supposed this second session of questioning was to clarify any possible discrepancy between Hung Doon's testimony and mine, although Hung Doon later did not seem to think there was any. Still, I do remember one snag: I could not initially remember the correct number of outhouses in the village. The same thing happened again in 1937 or 1938, when Hung Que came over. At Wing Lock's request I traveled by train to Seattle to offer testimony on behalf of Hung Que. The interrogation went well until I was asked the number of outhouses in our village. My answer turned out to differ from my paper brother's. Luckily that was not enough to deter Hung Que from landing. It was easy to foul up, especially if one was tired and was under intense pressure.

During my brief stay in the detention center some who had gone through this process told me that the interrogators were antagonistic and unrelenting, even downright rude. They pounded on the table to threaten the immigrants. They hurled curses, and fed the detainees misinformation to confuse them, so that they could break them down. I experienced none of that treatment. They treated me gentlemanlike and were helpful to me.[63] I personally did not harbor any fears of the interrogation; I was confident I would pass because I had thoroughly memorized the deposition book.

On the morning of January 3, 1936, they duly informed me that I had passed the grueling test, and that I could leave as soon as I had gathered my few belongings.[64] It was about 10:30 A.M. when I happily met Hung Doon at the detention center lobby.

Hung Doon and I left together and went to the Mar Don Hotel. He took me to see Mar Kuo King, my mother's number two sister's husband. Kuo King took us to a sumptuous dinner and handed me a twenty-dollar bill as a gift. My eyes widened at the sight of it; in those days that was a lot of money.

We stayed in cosmopolitan Seattle for two days. It was a pleasant, clean city, though choked with cars and rather hilly. Then we took a long train journey to languid Stockton, California. This is the locale where Hung Doon worked in a Chinese American restaurant before his recent return to China. Stockton was a prosperous farming community with a significant Chinese community. Most of the Chinese population there belonged to the Mar family from Taishan. I think Hung Doon dropped by the city to deliver a few messages from some countrypeople in China for their Stockton relatives. After a two-day stay we were on our way by train to Wichita, Kansas.

CHAPTER 2

☘ ☘ ☘   Life in Wichita, 1936–42

We arrived in Wichita on January 10, 1936. Two days after our arrival the city was hit by a severe winter storm—within hours seven inches of snow had fallen. The snow surprised me. Having lived all my life in a semitropical climate, I had never seen snow.[1]

I also had never seen such a large, well-furnished restaurant as the one my father and his partners operated. Leased from an American owner, the restaurant building on 150 North Market Street in downtown Wichita was three stories tall with hints of modern architecture, and was situated across from the impressive, beaux-arts-like, eleven-story Lassen Hotel.[2] The 118-seat restaurant occupied half of the ground-floor space, and a wallpaper and paint store occupied the other half.[3] The restaurant itself featured ornate tin ceilings, a long, well-polished mahogany counter with gleaming, leather-upholstered swivel chairs, and wooden tables with white stiffly starched tablecloths over them and well-padded wooden chairs.[4]

Most customers were white Americans. A number of them were transients or city visitors, while others were local regulars. Occasionally blacks showed up. They always entered the premises through the rear door that led to the kitchen. No waitress took their orders. Instead they just told the kitchen staff what they desired, and they would be served at a short counter set up in the kitchen just for them. When they were finished eating, they dropped their money into a tin can; typically the price of a black American's meal was half what customers in the dining room paid.

Throughout the day and night, and into the early morning hours, young Caucasian waitresses garbed in white uniforms with laced collars worked the teeming dining room. There was no such thing as writing down the orders, so they just yelled out the orders to the kitchen staff. Such a "system" came into being because the majority of Chinese workers did not know how to read English. Chinese workers—which included the partners of the restaurant—rushed about in the steamy kitchen, attired in sleeved white t-shirts, cotton trousers, long white aprons that extended well below the knees, and white caps. I suppose the language barrier made it difficult for the Chinese kitchen staff to wait on tables. Two of father's partners—Henry (Suey) Mar and King Mar, because they were the only ones who knew some English—dressed in ties and jackets and took turns ringing up the customers' checks.

Such a division of labor was fairly common. The other two Chinese restaurants in town before World War II—the Fairland Café and the Holly Café—also used white female waitresses and Chinese kitchen workers. Like my father's restaurants, those two also relied on countrypeople from the owners' villages, while the partners themselves were kinfolk.[5]

The second and third floors of that building consisted of uncarpeted partitioned spaces used as small sleeping rooms for the Chinese workers. There were altogether twelve rooms and two toilets, with washbasins on each floor. Shower facilities, or even a bathtub, were not available. To take a bath we relied on a water heater and a large movable metal tub. There were no cooking facilities for any of the rooms; they were unnecessary because the men took their meals in the restaurant kitchen. The rooms were sparsely decorated; only the necessary furniture such as beds, tables, and chairs filled these rooms. All of the rooms were occupied by Chinese men, both old and young. Workers of the Fairland Café also resided above the establishment, while those in the Holly Café resided in a rented building next to the restaurant—the arrangement was more convenient for them, but also downright cheap.[6]

There were no Chinese women in the city of Wichita at that time. Not until after World War II, when the Chinese veterans brought their wives to Wichita to start their families and raise children, did Chinese women appear in Wichita.[7] Until then the tiny Chinese community in Wichita was what we called a "bachelors' society." Of course they were not really bachelors. Either they left wives they had married before immigrating to America or sometimes journeyed back to China to marry the women, but then returned to the United States without them.

Their families left behind in China, the men in Wichita simply worked all day long, their fanciful dreams bound in a fading past. A typical day for the restaurant workers in the first shift began at 8:00 A.M. and rarely ended until past eight in the evening; those slated for the night shift worked just as long, starting at eight in the evening and ending the next morning at eight. Later in the 1950s a couple of the workers were slated from 10:00 A.M. until 3:00 A.M., although they took a short break in the afternoon. My father was one of those who pulled that long shift.[8] In 1936 there were three Chinese-owned cafés, and all were open twenty-four hours. The Wichita population stood at fifty thousand, while the Chinese population numbered about sixty, all male.[9]

I think it was a late Friday evening when we first reached Wichita. After checking out the new surroundings, and some aimless conversation with my father and a few of the coworkers, I turned in for the night, unfettered by any worries or anxieties. The next day, after a sound night of sleep, I went down to the expansive restaurant for breakfast. After a simple meal of thick rice porridge, salted fish, and preserved duck eggs, my father handed me a clean white apron. "Here," he said gruffly, "wash these bean sprouts." I also had to separate the husks from the mung bean sprouts, which I soon learned was one of the main ingredients of that quintessential American dish, chop suey. After I was done with this mundane task, Father—a bald-headed, genial-looking man, complete with a pudgy face, and yet possessing a no-nonsense approach to life—shoved a tub at me and ordered me to start bussing dishes.

After lunch, Father handed a few grubby dollars to a kindly, retired, scraggy-looking Chinese man, Wing Sen, who shared the room with Father, to help me buy some appropriate clothing. Wing Sen was an old-time sojourner who went back to China either in 1937 or 1938 to be reunited with his family, and then never came back to the United States. I saw him when I returned to China in 1946. I gave him some money to thank him for taking care of me when I was new to Wichita.[10]

That afternoon I bought school and work clothes, and longhandle underwear for the wintry weather. The new clothes fit me poorly. Father had instructed Wing Sen to purchase clothes several sizes larger than my current measurements. Father was always the thrifty one, but he was not a miser. For the next three exhausting hours we ducked in and out of numerous retail stores, looking for the best bargains, hoping to satisfy Father.

The following Monday, Wing Sen accompanied me to the public school—the Carleton Grammar School at 600 South Broadway.[11] I was thirteen years old. On the way Wing Sen explained to me how the traffic lights worked. He reminded me to always watch out for the hustle and bustle of the traffic. He jabbed me on the shoulder several times, insisting that I remember and recognize the landmarks and buildings so as to be able to find my way back to the restaurant. I ignored him, fascinated as I was with the new environment of tall, modern buildings, pedestrians garbed in the latest styles, and fast automobiles. Though I had been in cities before, Wichita struck me as unique—it was far less congested, and people moved slower. Fortunately, the school was a mere six blocks from the restaurant.

When I finally arrived at the school, it was quite an impressive sight. The school, built in the late nineteenth century, featured a combination of Romanesque and beaux-arts architecture. A tall tower jutted out from the main building. Students of various colors came from the nearby industrial district and the neighborhoods of the downtown district that featured rooming houses and apartment buildings.

In China I had received some English lessons from my village school-teacher. When I arrived in America I knew my alphabet and a few phrases. My English skills were admittedly still highly limited. For this reason, for reading class the staff entered me into the first grade, which seemed rather humiliating because I was already a teenager. These first-graders, though disheveled and rambunctious, did not snicker when they first saw me enter the classroom. I was quite surprised.

Looking back, I was glad they put me in the first grade for reading, because that was where I learned my basic English skills. I learned that every word must have a vowel, whether a long vowel or short vowel. Every day I had a new list of English words to become acquainted with and to memorize their spellings. I learned by writing the sound of the English word in phonetic Chinese. Initially I was mesmerized by the shape and sound of the English words, how each word went with a particular way of uttering it, so unlike Chinese, where many characters are pronounced as the same sound. Soon, however, what was intriguing became all too familiar. One can only have so much fun memorizing lists of words. For math they put me in the fifth grade, while for penmanship and geography they placed me in the third.

When school started for the new academic year in September 1936, the school staff placed me in the fourth grade for my reading class. I remember fondly one blonde, freckle-faced girl named Wanda Gibson. During recess the teacher, Miss Hull, allowed her to stay in the room to help me with my English. That was a big help, even though it felt "strange" receiving that from a nine-year-old girl. After that grade I had almost caught up with the rest of my peers. I spent a brief two and a half years at the grade school. All of the teachers were very helpful. Even their names—Miss Hull, Mrs. Wurtz, Miss Glenn, Miss Malone, Miss Williams, Mr. Berry, Miss McChristy, to name a few—sounded pleasant and welcoming. There were a few other Chinese boys attending Carleton when I was there. Fun Mar, Eck Mah, Lem Mah, and Jim Lee were sons of workers in the Mandarin Inn (later renamed Fairland Café) and Holly Café. Jim Lee was my age, and the others were younger. All of them had immigrated to the United States in 1935, and all of them hailed from Guangdong. Their fathers were American citizens, although they too were paper sons. Like myself, the boys started their schooling in first grade, even though they were several years older than their classmates. I hung out with these Chinese boys now and then, but work limited my interactions.

There was also eight-year-old Betty Mae Mar who was the niece of Mar Wah Sing, the owner of the Mandarin Inn, and the daughter of one of the workers there. Betty was different from us—she was born in Stockton, California, and her parents were born and raised in San Francisco. Betty did not even speak Chinese; she was easily the most Americanized of us all. Yet she did not help us with our English lessons.[12]

The most memorable event when I was still in the lower grades was that every Wednesday afternoon the class, accompanied by a devoted church volunteer, walked from Carleton School to the First Baptist Church at 216 East Second Street for religious education. This was my first formal exposure to the Christian faith. I did not think much of the experience; we sang hymns and read from the Bible—both of which I enjoyed—but the lessons never made much impression on me. In the fourth grade my religious education continued at the Methodist (now United Methodist) Church at 330 North Broadway. Again, someone from the church—not a teacher—picked us up from the school for the lessons. In later years my religious education was carried out at the Church of God on Second and Market Streets. The bible classes typically lasted for an hour, and then we would go back to school. I never attended church services on Sundays; endless work and the pace of my studies simply left me with little time for such ventures.

In the summer of 1938, at the recommendation of Miss Malone, my fifth-grade teacher, I attended summer school, which allowed me to skip the seventh-grade class and go on to the next one. I was an "old" student; I was keen to move on. Fortunately I was promoted from grade to grade until I reached ninth grade at the start of the 1940 school year. I spent a total of two and a half years at the Central Intermediate School at 324 North Emporia Street. I served on the student council. During my ninth-grade year I was the lieutenant proctor for the second floor. My teachers praised my conscientious work in these positions. Once I even delivered a talk at a weekly assembly program before the entire student body and faculty. I made straight A's in all of my classes. At the time I was a pretty good student.[13]

I also ran errands and did mundane tasks in the school office. Mrs. Marguerite Wiggins was the school secretary. She knew I did not have a family in Wichita, so she invited me several times to her house to have dinner and meet her mother and brother. Mrs. Wiggins told me, "Since you do not have a family here in Wichita, I'll be your *American mother*." This thrilled me. I enjoyed many fine dinners at her house.

Schooling exposed me to a new culture in the United States. Language, mannerisms, customs, and material culture—these were the new things I became acquainted with in school.[14] I learned English, common greetings, and about Christianity, Thanksgiving, Christmas, dating (though I never dated), and American food. The Chinese men I lived with in that restaurant building knew very little about the American way of life. All they did all day long was work and more work. They labored twelve hours a day, seven days a week. The men never went out; they just worked. They did their chores—sending money home, writing letters, washing their clothes. What little spare time they had they spent on mahjong, smoking, and daydreaming of the ones they left behind. Therefore they could not offer much help to me in my acculturation.

In retrospect I experienced very limited culture shock because at that tender age I probably changed with the culture. I never faced any discrimination in school. In my grade and intermediate schools there were a number of black students; in first grade, for example, there were five of them. Wichita had integrated schooling.[15]

My daily routine in those days from Mondays to Fridays was fixed, even rigid. In the mornings and afternoons, I attended school. After school I holed up in my room. Father had nailed together some pieces of wood and made a rickety bookshelf that soon buckled under the weight of all my books. He also found a dented, slightly wobbly table that I covered with a plastic tablecloth, and a chair he nabbed from the restaurant. Above the shelf, on the wall, I tacked the Chinese Nationalist flag I had brought with me from China, and an equal-sized U.S. flag I had purchased from a local dime-and-nickel store. A wooden bed with a thin mattress and a small wooden table completed the furnishings.

In this space I studied, making extensive use of the English-Chinese dictionary. I looked up every word in the dictionary to learn its mysterious meaning. My studies typically came to a predictable halt in the early evening. From 5:00 P.M. to 8:30 P.M. I toiled in the restaurant as a busboy, picking up dirty dishes, throwing away scraps, wiping off the tables, and resetting the table for new customers. After the dinner crowd had disappeared and much of the cleanup was over, I studied again until 11:00 P.M. On Saturdays and Sundays I did all kinds of back-breaking, arthritis-inducing kitchen work. I chopped the meat into small pieces, stripped and cut chicken, diced onions and potatoes, washed and trimmed vegetables, and occasionally cooked.

Dew Mar was another boy who worked at the restaurant. He came to Wichita in 1933, and was about three years older than I. Later Dew Mar was a medical student at the University of Kansas, in Lawrence, and then he was drafted into the armed services during World War II. He served in the Medical Corps. After the war he used the GI Bill to complete his medical education. As a boy growing up in Wichita, he spent his nonscholastic hours helping one of the cooks with the American fried food. My father cooked all the Chinese food, and I was assigned to help him.

Neither of us had much time for recreational activities; occasionally we joined a few Chinese youngsters from the other restaurants to play baseball in the nearby Riverside Park area, but such occasions were few and far between.[16] We did go to the movie theaters a number of times to watch cowboy films. A ticket cost only ten cents. I remember going to the Kansan Theater, Crawford Grand Opera House, and the Palace and Orpheum Theaters, all of which were in the downtown district. Whenever we went see a movie we sat on the main floor with whites; we did notice black and Mexican patrons in the balcony area.[17]

From 1936 through 1938 the Great Depression lingered on. A number of the Chinese-owned restaurants struggled through these times, as fewer and fewer customers dropped in. Father and his partners laid off a few of the waitresses and bought cheaper supplies. The workload eased up a little. The kitchen staff smoked and bantered more. The Nanking Café on 511 East Douglas bellied up in 1936, then someone took it over in 1937 and ran it as the Grand Café, but it failed within the year. By the end of the decade only the Pan-American, Holly, and Fairland Cafés were serving meals and ringing up the cash register.[18]

I remember a man in a car with sacks of potatoes filling the rumble seat. He tried to sell a fifty-pound sack of potatoes for one dollar. But the restaurant's chef said, "I will pay ninety-five cents." The salesman said, "No. I must have a dollar." So he left. Three hours later he came back and said to the chef, "I'll sell you a sack for ninety-five cents." He had driven around for three hours trying to get a nickel more. The gas he burned must have cost him more than five cents. The economy was that bad.[19] From that day onward I told myself that I was going to save my money, invest it, and let my money work for me.

Because these were hard times, Dew Mar and I worked at the restaurant for our room and board only. We received no pay. Looking back, I suppose one could argue that we were blatantly used, even exploited. But Father paid for all my clothing and personal needs, even my school supplies. My lodgings were free. Consequently, I bore very few expenses.

Of course, what little pocket money I received from him went a long way in those days. Lunch at the restaurant was twenty-five cents, which included a generous serving of meat, potatoes, vegetables, coffee or tea, and dessert. Hair cuts were fifteen cents. A gallon of gasoline was nine cents. Bread was five cents a loaf. Bus rides were five cents.

When school let out in June 1936 both Dew and I put in eight hours of toil every day for the rest of that dry summer. The Pan-American Café—as did the Fairland and Holly—operated as a partnership, so every month all net profits were divided equally among the partners. Even though these were hard times, the restaurant, as did the Fairland and Holly, raked in some profits because they operated long hours and could rely on a steady flow of customers from the nearby hotels. Some time in early June I overheard King Mar, the manager, talking to my father. He said that because "these boys" (Dew and I) were working every day, and the money never divided up evenly, he wanted to pay Dew and me a little bit of money. Because Dew had more experience than I did, the manager planned to pay Dew $10 and me $7 for the month of June.

From that point on they paid us the same salary every month, until June 1937. By then Dew and I both knew all about the monotonous kitchen work. Through the coming summer months we filled in as substitutes for the workers whenever they wanted time off. We received full pay, which was about $75 a month. In 1938 Henry Mar's boy, Ning, and King Mar's boy, Chin Wee, arrived in Wichita from China. Now there were four of us laboring in the restaurant.[20]

When Japan bombed Pearl Harbor on December 7, 1941, I was a studious sophomore at Wichita North High School on Thirteenth Street. Because that tragic attack took place early on a Sunday, I was still in bed fast asleep. After all, I typically worked late on Saturday nights. For me Sundays were the same as any other day; we usually anticipated a large after-church crowd, and would start later in the morning but work late into the early hours of the evening.

I first heard about the bombing of Pearl Harbor when I came down to the restaurant to work; the radio was on full blast and reporting on the atrocity. Everyone—from the well-coiffured if somewhat ruffled waitresses to the lowly busboys—was excitedly talking about it. Everyone was shocked.[21] The fact that the Chinese historically hated the imperialist Japanese intensified the reaction. I was stunned by the turn of events.

The next day, on my way to school, no pedestrians, or anyone else for that matter, glared at me or made any kind of inflammatory remarks. After all, I am Chinese, not Japanese. At school a special assembly was held to memorialize the loss. Nothing untoward happened; my classmates and teachers knew me well. The phrase "dirty Jap" was never mistakenly thrown at me.[22] I did deliberately buy a ring with an American flag on it, which I wore for years; I suppose I wanted to differentiate myself from the Japanese. If other Chinese people wore buttons bearing the slogan "I am Chinese," or displayed signs proclaiming "This is a Chinese shop," or carried identification cards issued by the Chinese Nationalist government, then my ring was just another way to prove my loyalty to the United States. Business at the restaurant remained the same; in fact, it became better as people gathered to dine and talk about the uncertain future. Soon, what happened on December 7, 1941, would shape my own life.

CHAPTER 3

♀ ♀ ♀   In the Army

In 1941 I was nineteen years old; I was short, no more than five feet tall, scrawny, and dateless. Life was a routine—school, work, and more work. News of the entry of the United States into World War II somehow evoked excitement in me.

That excitement was furthered by an event in town in 1941, before the Pearl Harbor attack. A liberty bond parade in Wichita on a very cold fall day found me, along with several other Chinese boys, sitting on a float sponsored by the restaurant.[1] We decorated it with small and large Chinese Nationalist and U.S. flags. The phrase "Buy U.S. War Bonds and Stamps" was printed all along the sides of the float. "United States" and "China," both in English and Chinese, were emblazoned on the float. As the float rolled down Douglas Street, the main thoroughfare for the parade, we waved at the crowds that thronged the sidewalks. People clapped and cheered. This was an enjoyable day.[2]

The thought of the draft was heavy on my mind. The minimum draft age was eighteen. All males age eighteen to thirty-five were required to report to the draft board and register.[3] Each draftee—depending on his number of dependents, physical condition, and type of current employment—was placed into a specific classification. A person who did national defense work might receive a deferment. Those who were physically unfit were classified IV-F.[4]

In September 1942 I was in my junior year at North High School. I was elected boys' vice president of the junior class. My ambition at that time was to pursue an electrical engineering career; the prospect of being a restaurant cook for the remainder of my life was unattractive. Therefore I enrolled in the second-year electricity class. I was now twenty years old. The next draft call could very well be for ages eighteen to twenty-five.[5]

My electricity instructor, Mr. Yoe, whose full name I cannot remember, was aware of the circumstances as well as my ambition. In October he told me he had received information from the United States Army Signal Corps that they had a new program called the Enlisted Reserve Corps (ERC). If a person enlisted in the corps he would receive eight intensive months of instruction at the Mechanic Learner Training School in Kansas City, Kansas.[6] The instruction would include radio theory and radio repair practical training. While a man was in training, the government would pay a munificent $85 per month to cover room and board. After the trainee had completed the program he would then be inducted into the regular army Signal Corps and serve in the communications department. The whole venture seemed to fit my ambition; the thought of a new adventure intrigued me.

Mr. Yoe gave me the application form to fill out. I quickly mailed it to the Seventh Service Corps in St. Louis, Missouri. On November 4 I received orders to report to Fort Leavenworth, Kansas, for enlistment processing. I passed my physical examination and was officially sworn in on November 6, 1942.[7]

Meanwhile, my father had returned to China in May 1941 to visit the family. Mother too returned to Changlong from her sojourn in Guangzhou. With war looming on the horizon, and rumors flying that the Japanese forces were poised to launch a major offensive deep into southern China, relatives in the villages eventually urged him to return to the United States. Father, however, convinced that he was needed at home, ignored the sage advice. The bombing of Pearl Harbor and the outbreak of war between the United States and Japan trapped him in Taishan for the war's duration. Fortunately, the Japanese occupied primarily the coastal cities, and our village was a fair distance inland.[8] My father could therefore turn his attention to farming and selling jewelry. This was his livelihood during the war years. Still, it was an unfortunate turn of events. Now I was on my own.

My number four uncle, Sai Jing Mar, and Wing Lock, my paper father, were now working in my father's restaurant.[9] Just before the war, at my father's urging, they had moved from California to Wichita. With three aircraft companies operating twenty-four hours a day the restaurant was busy all the time, and the demand for workers constant. Father needed the help, especially once he left for China.

There were all kinds of wartime price controls and rationing. The restaurant, however, was an old establishment with longtime, reliable suppliers. Local farmers, with their own small slaughterhouses, were able to supply meat and groceries, allowing the restaurant to meet its demand.[10]

Around December 10, 1942, I received my orders to report to the Kansas City training school.[11] I was fortunate to find room and board in a three-story house a mere six blocks from the school. The elderly woman who ran the boarding house charged $35 a month. For breakfast it was two eggs, toast and jelly, and coffee. For lunch it was always the delectable peanut butter and jelly sandwich to carry to school. Dinner consisted of roast beef or chicken stew or baked fish, with vegetable, potato, bread and butter, and dessert. The food was bland but hearty and plentiful. There were five white boys staying there who attended the same school, but I never got to know them. They kept to themselves. The landlady was courteous, if somewhat aloof, toward me.

Throughout my life in Wichita and the Midwest I faced very limited discrimination. Because this was the Bible Belt, most of the people were religious and were fair, kind, and helpful. I think the situation would have been different if I had lived in, say, San Francisco. Life would have been a lot more difficult in a larger city. The anonymity of big-time city life would have prevented me from getting to know people. Racial conflict, I understand, often prevented the Chinese from getting ahead. Had I lived in a large city I doubt I would have received as complete an education.

At Christmastime all the other boarders went home for the holiday season. I, however, had no home to return to. Christmas meant nothing to my father or his coworkers. However, a Lutheran minister called the rooming house landlady and found out I was the lone boarder still in town. He invited me to have dinner with his family.

On Christmas Day the minister came to the rooming house to pick me up promptly at 6:00 P.M. I brought a box of chocolate candy as a gift. We had roast beef and baked ham for entrées, vegetables, potatoes, gravy, hot rolls and butter, and dessert. It was a delicious dinner. After the hearty meal the minister and I sat down to chat about my life and family. While his wife finished washing the dishes and cleaning up the kitchen he took me on a nice leisurely drive to Kansas City, Missouri, for a two-hour sightseeing trip. It was about 10:00 P.M. when I reluctantly returned to the rooming house. Truly this was the best and nicest Christmas I ever had. Before this, Christmas usually meant a very busy and hectic workday at the restaurant.

During my training school I met another young man named Elmer Stuerke. He took me several times to Higginsville, Missouri, to spend the weekend with his family. To this day, over a span of fifty-eight years, we still exchange Christmas cards every year. I will never forget his kindness and his family's hospitality.

Besides Elmer and myself, there were an additional twenty-eight students in our class. Being young, all of us were obvious candidates for the draft. Therefore we decided to enlist for our choice of service. Four of the students already had two years of college. They were the outstanding students. I was the only nonwhite student, and so the only Chinese. Looking back I do not think I was self-conscious of the circumstances. I was confident I would do well in this program.

School started at 8:00 A.M. Every one and a half hours we had a rest break. Lunch was at 11:30 A.M. and class resumed at 12:00. School was out at 4:30 P.M. Every day was a long one.

During the first eight weeks they taught us the basic principles of electricity, geometry, and advanced algebra. I had a slight advantage over most of the students because I took geometry and basic electricity at North High School. In the second eight weeks, the morning class dealt with the principles of radio theory. In the afternoon class they taught us the basic skills of soldering, familiarized us with all the radio component parts, and also instructed us on the construction of a simple oscillator. At the end of the sixteen weeks, all of the students took a thirty-question test to monitor their progress. A few students, having flunked the test, were told to leave the school afterward.

During the third eight weeks we continued to have radio theory in the morning and workshop in the afternoon, with a little advanced training. We were now learning how to use the different radio test equipment, and how to analyze radio failure problems. At the end of the third eight weeks all of us took another test. A few more students were transferred out again. There were eighteen of us left to complete the training.

Officially on July 10 all of us had completed the Mechanic Learner's Training, and received a certificate attesting to that fact. The four students with two years of college were sent to Advanced Radio School in the east. Eight others were sent to Florida. On July 19, 1943, six of us were sent to Camp Kohler, the site of the Western Signal Corps training base.

Overall I was far from impressed with the training school. The first four months were good, but the last four were not very cohesive. On the classroom side the instructor who lectured on radio theory skipped certain chapters, mainly owing to the time crunch. We were not given any workbook or textbook to help us follow his lectures. Half of the time I did not understand what he was teaching.

To make matters worse, what was taught in the classroom was not extended to the workshop. The workshop was anything but that—it had woefully inadequate equipment. The school had four classes running simultaneously. A new class began every two weeks. The workshop sometimes would have two classes at the same time in the morning and two later in the afternoon. There was simply insufficient equipment to go around for all the students. Four or five students took turns using or studying a single piece of equipment. Most of the time we just milled around, chitchatting to kill time. I think they closed the school shortly after we graduated, because by that time the army Signal Corps base at Camp Kohler had the facilities and personnel to train all of their soldiers.

The train journey from Kansas City to Sacramento, California, was uneventful. Camp Kohler was near Sacramento. In July the daytime temperature sometimes shot up beyond one hundred degrees. The sun was intense but not any more so than in Wichita in the summer. At night the cold winds blew in, and we huddled under a blanket for cover.

At Camp Kohler I went through four intense weeks of basic training.[12] Every morning we did calisthenics before breakfast. We practiced marching in formation and crawling and running through obstacle courses, carried out overnight bivouacs, learned how to pitch a tent, received orientation on military codes and ethics, and tested for rifle marksmanship qualification. The grueling physical training took some getting used to; doing KP at 4:00 A.M. and then assembling for reveille at 5:00 was not easy. Neither was the routine of running for miles under the hot sun. The drill sergeant yelled at us all the time, even when we did nothing wrong. My daily routine back in Wichita, however, prepared me for this challenge. I did have a problem with my right eye, so I had to take the rifle marksmanship test the second time to qualify.

After three weeks of intensive, even hellish training, the platoon drill sergeant secured passes for anyone who wished to visit the town. All passes had to be approved ahead of time. Each soldier took his turn walking into the company office to receive it. The OD (Officer of the Day) sat behind a desk. You walked in, saluted, and said, "Sir, Private Wong requests for a pass to go to town." He returned your salute and said, "Request granted." Then he gave you the pass. You turned around, and stiffly walked out. It was that ritualistic.

Typically five of us—all Chinese—went to Sacramento together. There was a base bus to take us to town and bring us back. I remember that the incomparable Perry Como gave a concert at the convention center. We mostly sauntered along the streets, window shopped, enjoyed delicious Chinese dinners at little no-frills restaurants, and visited the USO (United Service Organization), which was open to all branches of the armed services, men and women. At the USO we listened to music, gobbled food that tasted far better than the grub we had been receiving in camp, and just milled around. Sadly we never danced with the American girls; we did not dare ask.[13] We typically returned to the base at about 11:30 P.M.

Toward the end of my basic training I met Henry Jin. All of five feet tall with gangly legs, Jin was from Brooklyn, New York. His English betrayed his origins; that accent was unmistakable. We became good friends. When we finished our basic training we promptly requested a three-day pass to go to cosmopolitan San Francisco. We were dying to escape the regimented lifestyle, at least for a short time. Our request was granted. We boarded a rickety old bus and rode to San Francisco together.

This was the first time I had ever been in temperate San Francisco, which the Cantonese called *Dai Fow* (First City). It was about 4:00 P.M. when we arrived at the overcrowded Chinatown, which then had the largest Chinese population in the United States.[14] We were looking for the Chinese Young Men's Christian Association (YMCA) to see if we might get bare-bones lodging for two nights.

We walked for a while, our unathletic legs almost ready to give way, as we peeked into the curio shops and smelled the aromas of roast duck, barbequed pork, and baked egg tarts wafting from the multitude of restaurants and bakeries, all the while sidestepping the overflow of boxes of vegetables and fruits that shopkeepers simply dumped onto the sidewalks. At one point we veered off from the commercial district and walked up a hill lined with Victorian buildings that housed Chinese residents in tiny apartments. Then we saw two Chinese girls walking downhill toward us. When we were close to each other, I said in Chinese, "Please excuse us. We are from Camp Kohler. Do you have a Chinese YMCA anywhere close by here?" One girl was about sixteen years old, the other about fourteen. Both of them were in bobby socks and long sloppy sweaters. The younger girl snapped at the older girl, "Don't talk to them, let's get out of here." Then she pulled the other girl to flee downhill. The older girl—the more svelte of the two—turned around to try to say something, but did not get a chance. I said to myself, "What a prude!"

Both of us, then in crew-cut hairdos, were in our smart-looking army uniforms with spit-shined shoes, so, in the girls' eyes, surely we could not have appeared to be bad people. The nervous-looking girls probably thought we were dishonest- or suspicious-looking characters, although how they could have arrived at that conclusion is beyond my wildest imagination. Still, they were unlike the people in the Midwest, who were helpful and friendly. It really made me appreciate the people in Wichita, Kansas.

It was about 6:00 P.M. when we walked to the main thoroughfare of the city, Market Street. People thronged the street and the sidewalks; the hustle and bustle of hectic city life was palpable. There we saw a huge, brightly lit PepsiCo, USO sign on an ornate building complete with colonnades and a portico in front. We approached the gleaming reception desk.

"Do you know where we can get a room cheap for the night?" I asked the pleasant-looking lady.

"Yes, we have two floors of beds here," she said sweetly.

"How much?"

"$2.00 a night."

"Great! Can we stay two nights?"

With a smile, she replied, "Yes." So we each gave her $4.00.

She handed us two paper cards with numbers scribbled on them. The whole floor was lined with roll-away beds with thin mattresses. They were all numbered. There were no partitions between the beds. Four big rooms housing the common showers and toilets made up the rest of the floor. These were bare-bones accommodations. Each guest, however, could come and go as he pleased. I understood these facilities were sponsored by the Pepsi Cola Company. The Pepsi beverage was available complimentary to the guests. This was good advertising for Pepsi. I bet this sensational service and free drinks converted many service personnel to buy and gulp down PepsiCo's product.

The next day we just aimlessly roamed Chinatown and tried many different kinds of delectable Chinese food. We took the winding trolley car to the expansive, shaded Golden Gate Park. Souvenir and food vendors were lined all along the beachfront, aggressively hawking their goods to gullible tourists and equally unsuspecting servicemen. We visited the seal rocks and had lunch there. I still have some pictures we took at the seal rocks. We returned to camp on Monday. I will never forget my first impressions of San Francisco and its Chinatown—both the good and the bad ones.

I suppose the Signal Corps trained its servicemen according to its varying, ever-changing needs. After basic training, they assigned me to the general clerical school for my specialist training. This assignment surprised me because I had undergone extensive training to be a radioman. Thirty-four recruits were enrolled in this "scintillating" class. The course included typing, filing, filling out military forms, lodging morning reports, updating 201 personnel files, keeping individual records for all government issues (such as clothing, shoes, equipment, and firearms), maintaining company property records, and clerical tasks.

Overall the course was hardly an obstacle for me. I already had one year of typing in ninth grade. I could type forty words a minute with ease. The course lasted only eight weeks; I think it ended on October 20.[15] I graduated at the top of my class and received a good recommendation from the instructor, a lieutenant. Frankly I did not learn anything new during those eight weeks that played a significant role in preparing me for my business life in the postwar years.

During this eight-week period, Henry Jin and I went to Sacramento a couple of times. We learned from other Chinese recruits that on Saturdays at the Young Women's Christian Association a Chinese group had reserved the time from 5:00 to 9:00 P.M. for Chinese GIs and women to meet and socialize.

Henry Jin and I attended one such meeting with great expectations. Attending were about fifteen Chinese high school girls, but there were about twenty Chinese GIs. Most of them, the GIs, were from Sacramento, so some of them knew each other. The hosts provided soft drinks, peanuts, popcorn, candies, and cake. Some attendees danced to recorded music, some played chess, but most simply sat, chatted, visited, and exchanged personal life stories. There was much conviviality in this setting.

At this party I met Wilma Fong. She was a charming, friendly, and vivacious girl. Most of the Chinese in Sacramento belonged to the Fong family. Her father operated two grocery stores in that city. She could not remember my name, but she remembered the state I was from, so she just called me "Kansas" all the time. "Hey Kansas!" she shouted with a gentle disposition. I asked her to have dinner with us, but she politely said she already had a dinner date. That was a major disappointment for us. We knew we would be shipping out soon, so we did not ask for her address or telephone number.

In the last few days of October 1943, Henry Jin, Harmon Wong Woo, Jimmy Kum, and I, without any forewarning, received orders to report for duty at Camp Crowder, Missouri. Harmon and Jimmy were from San Francisco.[16] The officials handed me an armband that said, "Acting Corporal," designating me the group's leader, and, along with that, a pouch containing our assignment orders, all our 201 files and clothing, equipment issue files, and the transportation and per diem vouchers. All of us wondered what awaited us in Missouri.

A U.S. Army truck took us to Sacramento and dumped us at the railway station to catch the train that took us all the way to Kansas City, Missouri. We were dressed in our smart uniforms, and everyone on the train was very friendly toward us. After several days of vistas that changed from mountains and hills to valleys and endless grasslands, the train finally pulled into Kansas City in the wee morning hours. When we woke up that cold morning, Harmon and Jimmy ducked their heads out the window and saw five to six inches of snow on the ground. They exclaimed, "I've never seen so much snow in my life!" During the rocking train ride they also marveled at the flatness of the plains, something I had never given much thought to. We waited all day long in Kansas City for the connecting train to Camp Crowder. It was about 10:30 P.M. when we reached our sprawling company quarters.

Camp Crowder was located in the southwestern corner of Missouri.[17] It was in a flat valley, but outside the camp was a large wooded area. It housed mostly the communications units brought to this place for advanced training. Men of all backgrounds and colors were here—white, black, brown, yellow. Joplin was the largest town near the camp and Neosho the closest little town.

Harmon, Jimmy, and I were assigned to Team 8. Henry Jin was assigned to Team 6. Kay S. Wong was the message center chief. He doubled as the supply sergeant. After I arrived I took over his duty as supply sergeant so that he could devote all his time to the role of message center chief for Team 8. Thomas Lew was our team chief. Lieutenant Thomas Hom was our team officer. All of us had been ERC students, and all of us were Chinese Americans.

We did not know of the existence of the 987th Signal Company until we arrived at Camp Crowder, and when I did learn of it I was surprised by the existence of not one but altogether ten similar units. The 987th Signal Company—activated on July 3, 1943—was entirely made up of Chinese-speaking American soldiers of Chinese parentage, and that included its officers. Even the company commander was Chinese. However, there were two exceptions—Lieutenant Hanken Lee was Korean American and Bernard Ring was a Chinese Italian American. However, we always considered them part of our unique unit and never saw them as outsiders. The company was the only all–Chinese American unit ever put together by the U.S. Army. There were other Chinese American units—altogether nine others—but they were part of the U.S. Army Air Corps, the forerunner of the modern air force. Specifically they made up the Fourteenth Air Service Group that provided technical assistance to the Fourteenth Air Force, better known as the "Flying Tigers," that flew heroic missions in the Chinese theater between 1943 and 1946.[18] Also, many of these units had white high-ranking officers, which differed from ours. All ten of the units eventually served in the China-Burma-India (CBI) theater.[19]

For the 987th Signal Company the plan was to have eight commissioned officers and 176 enlisted men. All of the enlisted men and officers spoke Chinese. Most of the enlisted men were initially assigned to staff an envisioned twenty radio-operating teams, each made up of eight men. The rest of the men made up the headquarters section. The company was organized expressly for duty in China. The unit eventually had the dual function of providing communication services and enhancing liaison between American and Chinese troops in that theater.

By the time I arrived, the company was pretty well into its operational status. The unit faced some initial problems that other non-Chinese units probably escaped. Some of the enlistees had only a rudimentary grasp of the English language, and thus encountered much difficulty keeping up with the technically driven specialist training. A few of the unit members volunteered to serve as interpreters and facilitate the teaching-learning process, but the exigency of waging a war that mandated rapid training forced out the men with weak language proficiency.[20]

Even though new men were brought in to replace those forced out, there were still too few enlistees to bring the company up to full strength. The company was then reorganized so that it had eight officers and 114 enlisted men, with the latter divided into ten radio-operating teams of ten members each, with the remaining men placed in the headquarters section.

The other challenge was that all of the enlistees in our company, including myself, spoke Chinese, but only the Cantonese dialect.[21] In China the Mandarin dialect prevailed. A person who spoke Cantonese could, in most instances, after a short course of instruction, learn to speak and understand Mandarin. A crash course in Mandarin was quickly put together and incorporated into the training program, using textbooks lent by several unit members. I never thought I would be learning Mandarin in the United States to go fight a war in China. The training, however, proved helpful, in more than one way, after the arrival of the company in China.

By the end of 1943 the majority of the company had completed specialist training. Radio operators and repairmen trained at the central Signal Corps school on the camp site, while other men received training for roles as message center chief, message center clerk, code clerk, motor mechanic, and truck driver. After the specialist training, the company was ready for the next phase: team training.

All enlistees, being soldiers who would be sent off to the war front, also received training on the use and maintenance of various weapons, such as sidearms, rifles, Thompson submarine guns, .50 caliber machine guns, rocket launchers, and grenade launchers. Some of this training was carried out in other U.S. Army facilities away from Crowder because the latter was in short supply of such sophisticated equipment. The men also received instruction in the use of auxiliary signal equipment such as signal lamps, signal flags, panels, and telephones. Most important, the men learned to operate in simulated combat conditions, employing camouflage, posting security guards, and even operating in blackout conditions. They pitched tents to house radio stations, set up the equipment, and communicated with different teams scattered within a radius of one hundred miles.

Harmon, Jimmy, and Henry blended in nicely with the rest of the team. I reported for duty at the supply room. I kept track of the individual records, took inventory, prepared requisitions, picked up supplies, checked in and returned the laundry, and maintained records of company property, all of which were the normal duties required of a supply sergeant. These were routine tasks, hardly the stuff that comes to mind for combat operations, but required for the proper functioning of the unit.

We celebrated Thanksgiving the week we arrived at Camp Crowder. Wichita was about a three-and-a-half hour bus ride away. I applied for a three-day pass to Wichita to see my relatives for Christmas. It was granted. Four other unit members went to Wichita with me; being from the West Coast they found Wichita amusing given its flatness and what they deemed a quaint downtown district.

Having left Wichita almost a year ago, I was delighted to see the men of the Pan-American Café. I learned from Wing Lock that my parents were coping well with wartime shortages and the threat of conflict in Taishan. I did not, however, have much of a chance to socialize with them; like the other two Chinese American restaurants in town, the Pan-American Café was jam-packed with hungry customers. The three aircraft companies were still operating twenty-four hours a day, so a wartime boom kept the food service industry humming.

An incident at Camp Crowder that I can recall—which Master Sergeant Thomas Lew, Henry, and Harmon were involved in—took place during a bivouac that marked the final phase of our training. For this bivouac, teams were assigned a general location and then told to scout around for a suitable spot, either on a public domain or a farmer's property, to set up their various tents.

One day during the course of this long exercise a jeep-load of enlisted men, along with an officer, drove into town. While parked on the main square of the town in front of a building, they suddenly found themselves descended upon by four burly characters converging from all sides and surrounding the jeep. The one who approached on the side of the lieutenant was obviously the sheriff; the others had "deputy sheriff" badges pinned on their coats. The husky sheriff wore the expression of an overfed cat who had just swallowed the flighty canary; he had maneuvered a successful capture of an elusive foe.

"Well, are you Chinese or you Jap?" the sheriff barked, with squinted eyes.

The Chinese lieutenant explained in a calm voice that they were Chinese but that they were also American soldiers in the Signal Corps.

"What are you doing here?" the sheriff demanded. "How did you get hold of all this army equipment? Why do you have a radio station set up out here in the woods?"

The Chinese officer elaborated that he and his men were on a training mission and were based at Camp Crowder, Missouri.

"Let me see your identification," the sheriff said gruffly.

All of the men showed their army dog tags. The officer turned over his identification card, which showed a photograph, signature, and official seal. In spite of the evidence, the sheriff was unrelenting.

"This card could be a forgery," he said in a snide tone.

The lieutenant suggested he telephone to get an officer from the Air Corps College Training Unit stationed at the nearby University of Arkansas to come and verify the authenticity of the card. While the men waited the sheriff and the deputies kept their eyes on them, with their hands resting on the triggers of their guns. After some time two Air Corps officers arrived. The entire explanation was dribbled out again, and the officers proceeded to check the card. Now, however, it was the turn of the big, strapping Air Corps officers to cast a suspicious eye on these short Chinese soldiers.

"How is it that you're all Chinese?" one of them snapped.

The officer told him that it was a unit made up of only Chinese American soldiers.

"But . . . don't you have a driver who . . .?" he said hesitatingly.

At that moment the officer finally understood the issue that was heavy on the mind of the Air Corps officer. So he jumped in and completed the question for him: "Are you trying to find a white GI to verify my identity?" he queried politely.

That Air Corps officer turned red in the face. He and the other officers then spoke quietly to the sheriff. Within a few minutes the sheriff approached the Chinese enlistees and dismissed them. They drove off, somewhat confused by the confrontation.

The story of this incident later went around the entire company; during those war years we feared being mistaken for Japanese spies or traitors. In retrospect this was an amusing incident, but at the time we did not think that was the case.

There was one other instance of discrimination at Camp Crowder that left a deep impression on me. On one occasion I went to a quartermaster warehouse to pick up supplies. When I walked in, two white supply sergeants and a black second lieutenant were already at the counter getting supplies. Thus I was fourth in line. The portly quartermaster sergeant, probably around fifty years old, took care of the first two whites, and then he turned to me. I was a corporal then, and not yet a supply sergeant.

"Corporal, what do you need?" the quartermaster drawled.

I looked at him, then looked at the black second lieutenant, then back to the quartermaster sergeant, somewhat unsure of what to say in reply. No one else said a single word. Silence reigned. Finally, still dumbfounded, I just handed over my requisition paper without saying a word. The sergeant amassed everything I needed, and momentarily I left in haste.

The second lieutenant was an officer and clearly outranked me. He was also ahead of me. Yet the sergeant took care of me before he turned his attention to the black lieutenant. The lieutenant for his part just stood there and did not say a single word. I suppose I was quite a lucky man not to be black.

The incident that probably left the deepest impression on me was what happened to my friend Harry T. W. Lew, who was a member of the 987th Signal Company. One weekend Sik S. Jung, also a member of the company, and Harry received a weekend pass to go somewhere for a change of scenery. They decided to go to Joplin. On the first day they had a nice dinner in a restaurant on Main Street and were really impressed with the quality of the food. The next day, which was a Sunday, they got up early but found that the restaurant would not be open for another hour. To kill time they decided to walk down the deserted street to check the train schedule for going back to camp later that evening.

They sauntered down the street, looking around like any other curious GIs who were in a new place. Neither of them noticed an unmarked police car with two policemen in civilian clothes. The car swung around rapidly and came to a screeching halt before the soldiers. The stocky officer on the passenger side jumped out and shouted, "You, what are you doing here?"

"What is the matter? We are going to the railway station," said Henry in a calm voice.

"Wise guys, huh? Let me see your pass," he demanded, still in a loud voice.

Harry looked at him in amazement, and replied, "Why should I show you our passes? We are American soldiers."

"Wise guys! You screwed our women and walked our streets. Now let me see how smart you are when we go down to the station."

Not seeing any identification from the officers, Harry said, "Who are you and why should we show you our passes?"

The other officer, much shorter than the menacing one, picked up the radio phone and reported that they had picked up two AWOLs (Absent Without Leaves).

Before Jung and Harry had a chance to figure out how to deal with this situation, the stocky one had already forced them into the unmarked car.

Arriving at the police station they were ordered to empty their pockets. Harry requested to make a telephone call to our company headquarters. The menacing officer snapped, "No! No calls!" Within minutes they were pushed into a cell—one with a cement floor, a toilet, a washbasin, and a small narrow window that opened onto the sidewalk outside. That was about 9:00 A.M.

Desperately they tried to figure a way to get a message back to our company headquarters. Lunch hour came. A woman pushed a pie pan of food and a tin cup of coffee through the cell door opening. After a while the two had to sit on the damp floor in their uniforms. Another four hours went by slowly. Then dinnertime came, with the same food and same server who glared at them with brows furrowed as though they were criminals.

Unexpectedly, a white soldier walked by their cell. Harry tried to convince him that they were locked up because they were Chinese. The soldier agreed to call company headquarters when he returned to the camp. Jung and Harry just kept their fingers crossed that he would not let them down. Each hour went by without any news. Their hope to be rescued began to fade and they tried to cope with the thought of spending a night sitting on a damp floor in a squalid jail.

Then about 10:00 P.M. they heard the voice of our company commander, Captain Victor S. Young. The soldiers shouted in unison, "Captain Young, we are here!" They overheard the captain saying to the night officer on duty, "I want to take my men out of the jail."

The night officer replied, "I could not find their names on the book. As far as I am concerned, they are not supposed to be here."

As soon as the soldiers heard that, they yelled as loudly as they could, "Hey! Captain Young, we are in here!"

After they were released from jail, Captain Young made this remark to the night officer: "You people just locked others for nothing." Jung and Harry left the police station relieved that they had survived the ordeal.

More lighthearted was the story of our company's consumption of rice. Because none of the units at the camp cared much for a heavy rice diet, we had access to an almost unlimited supply. The mess officer and mess sergeant contrived to serve strictly Chinese dishes several times a week, using the quartermaster-issued rations. That in itself was quite a feat. The reputation of these meals soon spread to other units. Non-Chinese soldiers soon showed up at our mess hall at opportune moments. Suddenly comrades became friends. To keep ourselves from starving, we had to disappoint many interlopers.[22]

All things were progressing well. By the end of March 1944 all the training had been completed, and our company was declared ready for overseas duty in the CBI theater. Soon we received the orders for overseas duty. Everyone was given one week of furlough.

Ever since I entered the service Moy Jing had been taking care of my savings. Because I was in a communications company, I was unlikely to be caught in the line of fire, so my chances of returning from the war were good. Hence I asked myself what should I do with my $1,200 savings. At that time, the Beech Aircraft Company's stocks were worth about $10 a share. I could afford to buy one hundred shares. I also, however, wanted to visit China to see my mother after the war.

Eventually I wrote to the Bank of China, which had a branch in New York City, to see what kind of Chinese war bonds or investments were available. I rationalized that such a move on my part would be a contribution to the anti-Japanese war effort. After all, I expected China, with a helping hand from the United States, to win the war. I was thus confident that my investment would reap profits. Furthermore, when I did travel to China for my visit I would have Chinese money to spend. The exchange rate quoted by the Bank of China was $5.20 U.S. to $100 Chinese. On December 1, 1943, I sent $521 to the Bank of China for a

$10,000 Chinese savings account that bore 8 percent interest per year, with compound interest every six months.[23]

In May 1944 I found myself busy getting ready for overseas duty. First Lieutenant William Ching was the supply officer. He and I left Camp Crowder on May 26, five days ahead of the troops, as the advance party to Camp Anza, near Wilmington, California, which was also the port of embarkation. We rode in luxurious first-class Pullman accommodations, which converted into beds with soft, high-grade cotton linens. We arrived at Camp Anza on May 30.

The company left Camp Crowder on June 1, 1944, by troop train, packing the soldiers tightly, because space was limited. Hard, wooden benchlike seats did little to ease frayed nerves. The troops, fatigued but in high anticipation, arrived at Camp Anza on June 4, 1944. The following week was a hectic one. Every soldier was issued all the various sets of clothing and equipment needed for overseas duty. India—which we would stop at en route to China—is hot and humid, so we would need light, summer-oriented clothing. Kunming, China—where we were told we would be based—is at a higher altitude, and it would be winter when we arrived there, so we were also issued heavy, typically woolen clothing for that season.

We tried on our new clothing but found, much to our dismay, that it was ill-fitted for our bodies. The sleeves were a little too long, the trousers a little too large.[24] The army had made no provisions for the differences in physical features between Asians and non-Asians. All of the enlisted men received the Garland rifle. The officers carried the carbine. The company possessed two .50 caliber machine guns, ten rocket launchers, and twenty-four grenade launchers.

Every person was examined by a health officer before he could leave for duty. When the health officer—a bespectacled, lanky captain with unusually large ears—examined me, he asked me to raise my hand and rotate my shoulder. Then he looked puzzlingly at my eyes, and barked, "Something wrong with your eye?"

I admitted, "Well, I can see only with just one eye you know. And when something is out of the sight of my right eye, I can't see."

Then the doctor pointedly asked, "Soldier, do you want to get out of the army?"

"No," I said firmly. "I've been training with all these men here and I want to go overseas with them."

In a matter-of-fact tone, he replied, "OK, alright, you have your choice."

I chose to go overseas with the rest of the American soldiers because I really wanted to go see China. I wanted to have the experience of going abroad. I also wanted to serve my country, the United States, while aiding China in its long struggle against imperial Japan. I had heard and read about the Japanese atrocities in Nanjing and other Chinese cities in the years before the sneak attack on Pearl Harbor. Both China and the United States faced a formidable enemy. I rationalized that every able-bodied man should contribute to this war effort, and so must I.

All of us were given six immunizations. On the first day we received three jabs, and two days later we suffered three more. All this on top of the detailed physical examination.

We also attended several lengthy, "stimulating" orientation lectures. One was about personal health and hygiene; we were told not to drink tap water but instead to drink the boiled variety, or water that had been processed through a chemical filter. "Be wary of local foods," the officer warned. "Eat your K rations when in doubt," advised the officer. Someone behind me muttered, "and enjoy the 'gourmet food'." We also became acquainted with the nature of mosquito bites. We heard talks about the cultural, religious, and language differences between the United States and China. For most of us, that struck us as odd—after all, we were Chinese! We were Chinese Americans but still grew up in the Chinese community. We knew at least some of its culture, traditions, and mores. Most of us were somewhat apathetic toward these lectures; we were too consumed by the thought of the uncertain future.

The army made us watch the film *Baptism of Fire,* which was roughly one hour and fifteen minutes long. In hushed silence we watched a film that depicted intense front-line battle, particularly hand-to-hand combat scenes. I suppose this was one way of preparing us mentally and psychologically for the eventuality of life-and-death situations.

We left the West Coast on June 8, 1944. Embarkation took place in total darkness owing to security reasons. Our transport ship was the SS *Gaillard,* which carried four hundred troops, which was at least one hundred more than its normal capacity. It was heavily loaded with war materials, with three airplanes tied down on the top deck. Our bunk beds were six decks high.

Needless to say, we were packed like sardines. We gasped for fresh air; every morning the men scrambled up to the deck for gulps of fresh air. By sundown everyone had to go below except for the crew members. At night, ship hatches were closed; should torpedoes have hit the ship, then damage to the ship and personnel would have been minimal.

Another common rule was that smokers were not allowed on the top deck, because a light could be seen for miles by the enemy. Because I never smoked, this rule hardly concerned me; still, we were aware of the perilous circumstances of our journey across the wide Pacific.

When the ship was pitching and rolling, clanging and banging, sleep was almost impossible. The foul air below the deck hardly helped. When the ship reached the Indian Ocean, conditions in the hold were unbearable. It was hot and sticky—at 130 degrees with humidity around 100 percent. To prevent anyone from suffering heat prostration, most men slept on deck under the wings of the fighter planes securely tied down. I heard that in other Chinese American units that traveled to India, hammocks were hung over the dining area.

When the ship was passing through the Tasmanian Sea near Australia, the ship was moving violently, pitching and rolling side to side. The bow and stern were churning up and down with waves at fourteen to fifteen feet high. I doubted the ship's speed could have been more than three knots per hour. It was the first and only time in my life that I saw flying fish. The fish flew fifteen feet high out of the water, and then dropped back into it with a big splash.

For three days in a row the mess hall was deserted. Normally the mess hall served three shifts for each meal. Seasickness did not bother me. I was one of about sixty people in the mess hall and we ate to our hearts' content. Of course the daily fare was nothing to rave about—it consisted of powdered eggs, baked beans, and the famed "SOS" ("Same Old Shit," which was gravy with bits of meat over the biscuits).

On July 16, 1944, our ship arrived at its first port of call: Freemantle, Australia. We were ecstatic with this pleasant diversion after being cooped up in the hold for thirty-eight days. Our whole unit obtained an overnight shore leave and was able to visit and go sightseeing in Freemantle or Perth. The scenery was captivating and the weather mild and balmy. Perth was the better and larger city, so we spent more time there.

The first thing that caught our eyes when we reached downtown Perth was the restaurant sign "Little Toishan"[25] in both Chinese and English. Most of the Chinese soldiers in our company were from Taishan. We instantly filled up that restaurant, which we would call today a "hole-in-the-wall," excited by the prospect of eating some authentic Chinese food, any real food. The restaurant was owned and operated by a nuclear family—an uncommon scenario in the United States before World War II, but apparently not so in Australia. The father and mother slaved in the kitchen while their two girls in their late teens waited on customers in the sparsely decorated dining room. They did not expect this kind of business volume at one time. We were the unanticipated deluge. They ran out of food well before everyone was fed, and had to rush out to buy more ingredients.

About thirty of us went back for our second meal before we returned to the ship. Earlier we were too engrossed in gorging on the roast duck, steamed dumplings, and stir-fried vegetables, along with lots of fragrant rice, to notice anything else. On our second visit the pace was more leisurely, and then we had the opportunity to visit with the girls. We chatted with them; they laughed and giggled most of the time. Their surname was Wong. They were from the Taishan county seat of Taicheng. Too bad we were leaving soon for the war front; otherwise, we would have enjoyed getting acquainted with them.

Our ship left Freemantle on July 19. It took three full days to replenish all the fresh water, provisions, and fuel and do all necessary repairs. When we left the United States our main dish was beef, or more like bits of it. Now our main dish was lamb. Every day, we had either roast leg of lamb or lamb stew—a reflection of the popularity of this meat in Australia. We soon grew tired of it.

The men aboard the ship had experienced a "sub scare." One night they saw a huge whale that was nearly as long as the ship; the whale even swam alongside the ship for some time. Naturally, our first thought was that it was a Japanese submarine. Fortunately, we encountered no such incidents, made all the more remarkable because the ship made the passage alone without escort or convoy. Our ship, however, did have radar to detect and evade enemy submarines.

Not so lucky was the tragedy of the SS *Jean Nicolet*. One postwar report noted that this troop ship left Wilmington, North Carolina, twenty-one days ahead of our ship. Traveling the same route and headed also to Calcutta, the *Jean Nicolet* was torpedoed by a Japanese submarine off the coast of Australia. Some seventy-seven men immediately lost their lives. The survivors were captured as prisoners of war, but then forced to run through a gauntlet of clubs and bayonets wielded by menacing Japanese sailors. An unidentified airplane, however, sent the Japanese submarine scurrying to go underwater, leaving the few plucky survivors to fend for themselves, though they were rescued some fourteen hours later.[26]

After traveling sixty days, including the three memorable days at Freemantle, we finally arrived in Calcutta, which was, however, not the disembarkation port for most of the Chinese American units. For most Chinese American units the disembarkation port was Bombay.

Our unit was staged at Camp Kanchrapara in the foothills near Calcutta. Tea plantations and fruit orchards dotted the scenic landscape. Kanchrapara essentially was a temporary tent camp for a number of the units—not just ours—before the final journey to China.[27] Here all of our team members underwent further specialist training at the U.S. Army Post Signal School. Radio operators became more familiar with the Pilot Radio Corporation's model V-100 radio, the set most extensively used in the CBI theater. Message center people were instructed in the double transposition cipher, which was also in extensive use. While all radio team members underwent more training, the headquarters personnel—and that included myself—did not have much to do.

It was the monsoon season. It rained every day. After the pouring torrents, the sun reappeared, and soon the earth was baked. It was hot and humid. At sundown all the men applied mosquito repellent. Though we were mindful of drinking only purified water, several men did catch malaria while stationed there.

There were a lot of jackals; they howled constantly all night long. There were a lot of snakes too. Oftentimes at night when you pulled

back your blanket to crawl into bed—and as luck would have it, mine
featured a broken spring—there was one such reptile under the covers
ready to do battle with its unwelcome guest. Creepy giant earthworms
also found their way into our boots.

The food was terrible. India could not feed its own people (and it
still cannot), so there was no extra food to feed the Allied army. Most
of it had to be imported. The cow was sacred, and not to be slaughtered
for food. Meat was scarce. For breakfast it was powdered eggs every
day, and it tasted like sawdust in our mouths. For lunch and dinner we
had baked beans without the pork, and rocklike biscuits. Occasionally
the cooks served fried Spam and hot dogs; when such food appeared,
there was a rush for seconds. Many of the men in the various units
went to nearby towns to buy greasy fried chicken, fried rice with pork,
or something else when food was unpalatable in the camp. We stayed
at Camp Kanchrapara for six weeks—it was the longest period in my
life.

Several of us got together and ventured into Calcutta three or four
times. Calcutta was an old city—poor, dirty, overcrowded, and dotted
with dilapidated buildings. People slept on sidewalks and in the streets.
Everywhere I turned I saw beggars with outstretched hands and eyes
that yearned for another life. I have never seen any other people in such
a desperate plight.[28]

Our company left Camp Kanchrapara on September 19, 1944, traveling by narrow-gauge railroad and riverboat to Chabua, Assam, where
a large air base and river port were situated. We traveled for the next
seven or so days in railroad boxcars. The trip on the railroad car was
highly uncomfortable. We loaded our gear, supplies, and equipment
onto the train in the humid heat while still garbed in our heavy khaki
uniforms and toting our guns. Onboard the train we had to share very
limited space with chickens, goats, and people. The hard seats allowed
little sleep. Whenever the train made a stop we filled our canteens with
boiled water. Dysentery was a serious health problem, and we were
mindful to avoid that risk to our bodies.

The riverboat ride to Chabua was no more pleasant; the boats were
old and rusty. Space constraints forced the men to huddle together.
From Chabua we were airlifted in unarmed transport—I believe it was

a C-46, also called the "flaming coffin"—over the "Hump" to China.[29] The flight took about four to five hours; this was a memorable trip in the worst way. The Hump was a treacherous air route—our transport plane bobbed up and down as we constantly hit air pockets, even as it tried to circumvent high mountains and avoid the attention of enemy planes. Several times the plane shifted altitude at thousands of feet within a minute. Fortunately, our plane never flipped over. A couple of the men threw up—a reaction for which they received incessant ribbing. During the war years a number of these transport planes, which lacked speed and maneuverability, crashed while flying this route, either from taking fire from Japanese fighters or, more often, the victim of inclement weather.

The unit arrived in Kunming, Yunnan, on October 1, 1944, and was headquartered at "Hostel 9," which truly consisted of large tents and nothing else. Things were somewhat primitive in Kunming; until just before we arrived, there was not even any electricity, but supposedly some ingenious Chinese American soldiers had found these disused one-horsepower engines and rigged them as generators. In Kunming the men of our company underwent more training in the use of the V-100 radio and double transposition cipher.

The minute I stepped off the transport plane I felt and smelled the fresh crispy air in Kunming. High and desolate, Kunming was in a province that bordered the British colony of Burma, and for a long time the French, who ruled Indochina, used it as a hill station to escape the humid, tropical climate farther south. Surrounding the city of one hundred thousand residents were jagged mountains with limestone caves carved into them, hillsides with terraced rice fields, rapidly flowing wide rivers, and several lakes. Grass-covered valleys, dotted with sun-dried mud houses connected by narrow dirt roads, also formed part of the stupendous countryside vista. Poplars grew here and there. Within the city, houses featured brick walls and tiled roofs.

The tranquil surroundings, however, offered a mirage. Kunming housed four separate air bases that Chinese laborers built using hand tools, and were laid out some miles away from the downtown area. It was also the headquarters of the Fourteenth Air Force. The Japanese knew of Kunming's strategic importance. During my stay in Kunming numerous air-raid sirens went off. Whenever that happened we grabbed our guns and jumped into the foxholes. Luckily, no menacing bombs ever dropped on us.

Food was plentiful at Kunming. For breakfasts we had real eggs from nearby farms. For dinners we often had pork chops with homegrown vegetables and potatoes. Occasionally chicken was available. At the very least we had one hot meal each evening. We still ate our K rations, but at least that no longer dominated our diets. Some entrepreneurial men traded their Red Cross–supplied cigarette rations for chicken and vegetables from local vendors. It was a world of difference compared to the food we had in India.

For leisure the men often ventured into Kunming to socialize either at the USO building or the Red Cross establishment, the Town Club. In those places the men smoked and drank, listened to records, read newspapers and magazines, played cards, bingo, and dominoes, and exchanged tall tales of each other's wartime exploits. Popular Hollywood versions of the war, such as John Wayne's *The Flying Tigers*, were also screened. Some men also shopped at the noisy and chaotic Thieves Market, where aggressive vendors pressed their dizzying variety of wares on unsuspecting, gullible GIs. All sorts of things, ranging from priceless Chinese porcelains (sometimes fakes) to hard liquor, were available for a price.[30]

In Kunming I received the biggest shock in my life when I learned of the exchange rate of $1 U.S. for 300 Chinese dollars. The $520 U.S. I used to set up a 10,000 Chinese dollars savings account had plummeted in value down to $33 U.S. By the time we returned to the United States on October 8, 1945, the Chinese treasury note was practically worthless, trading at a rate close to $1 U.S. for 2,000 Chinese dollars, and by then, of course, no one cared for it. (These Chinese notes were issued in 100, 500, 1,000, 5,000, and 10,000 notes.) So the Chinese treasury came out with a new kind of currency, and the notes were supposed to be guaranteed and backed by the receipts from the custom duties. I believe the currency was put into circulation in January 1945. I do not remember the exchange rate when the currency was first issued. When I went back to China in June 1946 it was akin to $1 U.S. for 300 Chinese dollars.[31]

The headquarters personnel were among the first group to leave Kunming in the middle of November and report for active field duty at Kaiyuan, Yunnan, which served as the Southern Command headquarters area. The Southern Command covered all of the southern Yunnan Province to the French Indochina border, which was then occupied by the Japanese.[32] The other men in our company followed in the next ten days or so.

In Kaiyuan our company was broken down into small detachments to be two- to four-man radio operating field teams responsible for communications for the U.S. Army's Infantry Liaison teams attached to the Chinese army divisions and regiments guarding the French Indochina border.[33] Elements of the company then fanned out along the extent of the French Indochina front, about seventy miles in width and fifty feet in depth.

After March 1, 1945, when the 26th Signal Center detachment was transferred to another assignment, the company became solely responsible for communication of all echelons on the southern front, from army headquarters to regimental command posts, altogether comprising about thirty-five separate installations. In sum, the company was the sole manager and operator of the communication system for Allied ground forces in the region. Because of the tactical disposition of the liaison troops, it was impossible as well as unnecessary to keep the ten-men teams intact.

The company later also provided communications for several reconnaissance patrols that penetrated southward deep into the Japanese-occupied Indo-Chinese territory during the 1945 Chinese offensive.[34] Pack mules carried the V-100 patrols, with one radio operator and one code clerk traveling with each patrol. These patrols, fortunately, managed to escape the eyes if not the knowledge of the Japanese, and no casualties resulted from enemy action, though often fast mobility was necessary.

The company headquarters were maintained at Kaiyuan. Our headquarters group at Kaiyuan consisted of the company commander, a captain, the supply officer, a first lieutenant, a first sergeant, the company clerk, a supply sergeant, six in the motor pool group, two mechanics, four truck drivers, the mess hall group, and one mail clerk. Our company mess hall personnel took over the headquarters officers' and enlisted men's mess hall. It was established that the officer group would be served first, followed by the enlisted men. The motor pool personnel pulled duty with the Southern Command motor pool personnel. Our mail clerk—whom I assisted now and then—delivered mail to the dispersed front-line troops.

I was the company supply sergeant, whose primary duty was to keep an accurate account of the company properties and to safeguard them at all times. In that capacity, I had to keep an up-to-date file record of all items of clothing and equipment issued to the soldiers. I made requisitions for everything the company needed and kept track of the inventory.

During my service in China, supplies were often hard to come by. Radios, guns, vehicles, medicine—everything was in short supply. Mechanics often had to cannibalize old radios or salvage old parts to make equipment operable. The basic soldiering skills we learned in training school came in handy now. Sometimes even flat tires could not be repaired. The only things we had plenty of were Spam cans and K rations, stacks and stacks of them. Because we had access to fresh vegetables and meat we rarely ate Spam or the K rations. Oftentimes we also received Red Cross packages that contained cigarettes, reading material, and candy bars. These were precious "commodities" because the men often traded them in the Kaiyuan market for fresh food.

The delay in receiving the supplies resulted from the state of the local economy. Wrecked trucks were abandoned on roads because of the shortage of spare parts or because of the use of alcogas, a very poor fuel. Meat was often spoiled or rotten because the Chinese did not meet basic sanitary conditions for abattoirs. The inflation rate, most of all, limited our ability to get goods and services in the open Chinese market.[35] Frank D. Leong, the founder of the Flying Tigers Memorial (see Chapter 7), recalled hauling hundreds of tin containers of worthless notes from Kunming to Luiliang to pay Chinese labor contractors.

Besides handling administrative and tactical communications, our unit also published daily news bulletins. Several men at the Kaiyuan headquarters collected and edited news from British Broadcasting Corporation press releases and broadcasts from U.S. radio stations and the army station in Kunming. Such news bulletins often served as the only source of information for many installations. A shortage of paper often hampered the dissemination of the much-sought-after information in this isolated region.

Some of our personnel also aided in conducting signal schools for the Chinese army. Our officers planned courses of instruction and, together with the enlisted men, served as instructors. At these schools the Chinese soldiers were taught field wire equipment and construction, switchboard procedure, radio code, and the operation and maintenance of radio and wire equipment. The ultimate goal of the training was to produce skilled wire construction men and field radio operators for the Chinese army.[36]

Initially the Yunnanese dialect (a variant of Mandarin) posed a communication barrier for our company members because most of the men spoke Cantonese of the Taishan variant. Even the language training we had received at Camp Crowder did not prepare us for this setting because we had been taught Mandarin of the Beijing dialect. Therefore at first we relied on local interpreters to carry out the instruction.

Gradually some of our instructors did understand more of the local language, and they were then able to converse with and provide instruction to these Chinese troops. The instructors were delighted with their fairly rapid mastery of the language because these few could then commence liaison with the desirable female elements of the local community. As it turned out, however, the non-Chinese-speaking members of the U.S. Army were performing just as efficiently without the benefit of Mandarin.

As for me, I found Chinese troops very different from us. They were poorly equipped and poorly dressed. Some of the foot soldiers did not even have shoes. Compared to the Americans, the Chinese were ill trained and lacking in discipline. Language also limited my interactions with the Chinese rank-and-file; however, I never faced any difficulties from them.

The weather at Kaiyuan, Yunnan, is mild year-round. There was no snow in the winter, and as such, it was just like the conditions in Taishan, Guangdong. Even at night in the winter months the weather remained cool and pleasant. Sacramento comes to mind for comparison because Yunnan also enjoys a planting season of nine months. The hard-working farmers could reap three bountiful harvests in a year if the conditions worked out.

All of us lived in tents with canvas cots. The company commander and the supply officer stayed in one tent. The company office, where First Sergeant Edwin Howe and Company Clerk Henry Chau also slept, was the next tent. I worked in the third tent, which stored twenty boxes of spare radio parts. The fourth tent was where Edwin Howe, Henry Chau, and I lived. The fifth tent housed the motor pool made up of Sergeant Henry Wong, Gene H. Lee, and Walter Ring. Because all our radio team members were out in the field, there was not much work for any of us in the headquarters.

We stored all the company's munitions, machine guns, rocket launchers, grenade launchers, and radio equipment in a 12 ft. x 15 ft. brick building whose door had a sturdy lock. It was my responsibility to check the padlock every morning to see that it was secure. However, the shortage of supplies meant that the building was rarely filled up. This building, as well as others in the vicinity, was furnished by the Chinese army, which had requisitioned existing civilian houses and buildings for the exclusive use of the American liaison troops.

Every morning Chinese soldiers brought us hot water for cleaning up. They picked up our dirty laundry every Sunday, washed it, and brought it back. There was very little conversation between the American and Chinese soldiers; I think the language barrier was the reason.

Life was pretty easy for us at the headquarters. It was almost a vacation. There was a day room where we could congregate and play the popular Chinese pastime mahjong. At the so-called 21 Club—which actually was a tent for the men to socialize in—we could partake of liquor and wine. I had heard that in other units based in China the men organized their own basketball and baseball teams. A few men even brought their own musical instruments and formed a jazz ensemble to entertain the local women; alas, there were no such talented people in our unit.[37]

It was only a five-minute walk into the town of Kaiyuan. It was a small settlement of simple concrete buildings and rudely constructed shacks, and one or two pagodalike structures situated along a railroad that in turn led to Kunming, which was on the route to the French Indochina city of Hanoi.[38] I estimated that about nine hundred to one thousand people lived in this town on a permanent basis.

On market days the town came to life—it could get rather noisy and crowded. All kinds of enterprising vendors—grubby, unwashed, and yet always pleasant—showed up to hawk their merchandise. They sold many different kinds of fruits, vegetables, clothing, handicraft items, herbs, spices, wild game, and meat. The market typically drew around three hundred people from the surrounding countryside to town for shopping. Local Chinese residents jostled with U.S. servicemen and indigenous Yunnan people for the goods. I saw many Miao people dressed in their intricately designed traditional clothes. Their women were adorned with colorful bead jewelry and were topless.

The people in Kaiyuan spoke their native dialect and the Mandarin language. We spoke the Cantonese dialect. Therefore, our mingling with the local people was fairly minimal, beyond the smattering of words and phrases we had picked up and the use of nonverbal signs. However, whenever we went into the town or the countryside—and we were readily identifiable because we were always garbed in the U.S. Army uniform—the Chinese population invariably gave us the thumbs-up sign and said in their local languages that "America is very good." To me, this was a recognition of our role in the war; we were American soldiers waging a good war half a world away.

War created many desperate refugees and forced them to flee to a safer place, such as Kaiyuan. The town population swelled to thousands for months at a time. Existing primitive conditions—the absence of running water and outhouses, for example—turned into health hazards with this upsurge in the population. The poverty in Kaiyuan was obvious; children in ragged clothing often held out their hands for food and coins.

I became closely acquainted with one sundry store owner in town who had fled from the Guangzhou area; I visited and patronized his store quite often. Other Chinese American soldiers and I bought sundry items from him and chatted up his attractive, well-mannered daughters. We also exchanged with him colorful stories about life in prewar

Guangdong. Through him I met some other people from the Guang-dong area.

There were a few memorable events during our stay in Kaiyuan. George Eng, our company mail clerk and a reckless driver to boot, delivered the highly anticipated mail to the men out in the field, and so had ready access to an army jeep. He was the envy of many of the men. That vehicle also gave him the opportunity to go to places to meet other people.

He became acquainted with a woman, Ann, who taught grade school at a nearby Kaiyuan village. Her brother was a colonel in the Chinese army. They were war refugees who originally hailed from Guangdong. George and Ann fell in love and were married in May 1945 in Kai-yuan. They threw a big French-style wedding banquet that featured an eighteen-course meal. After the war, George and Ann returned to Guangzhou and operated two sundry stores. In 1946 I returned to Guangzhou. Walking on one of the streets, I suddenly spotted George standing in front of one of his stores. I was quite surprised because I was working with the assumption that he had returned to the United States following his army discharge. George and Ann later fled to the United States just before the Communist victory in 1949.

I had an uncle (my mother's sister's husband), King Mar, who lived in Seattle. During the war years we corresponded several times. Through him two of his relatives from Kunming—specifically, two attractive, petite distant cousins in their early twenties—came to Kaiyuan to visit me for three days.

From that meeting they arranged for me to meet Colonel Mar at Kunming in October 1945. Colonel Mar, my mother's brother-in-law, was a Nationalist army transportation officer based in Chongqing, a city that housed a lot of refugees who fled the Japanese occupation of China's coastal regions. I think Colonel Mar joined the Nationalist army on his own accord; China was his country of citizenship. It seemed natural for him to support China in the hour of its greatest need. For me the meeting with him turned out to be a joyous one because he was the closest relative I had encountered since my departure from the United States.[39]

In fact, during the war years I was in very limited contact with my family members, both those in China and the United States. I did not write to my father and mother, who were then living in China. Perhaps they did worry about me, but we never talked about their concerns. They never knew I was in China until the war was over. I did not know whether it was safe for us to communicate behind the bloody Japanese line. Besides, the censorship of letters would have certainly curtailed the amount of information I could share with them. I also rarely wrote home to Wichita. I only wrote to my paper father, who was running the restaurant in Wichita, to get him to help manage my finances. I do not think my paper father worried too much about me because things were so hectic in his restaurant business. I learned that other Chinese American servicemen did send letters, remittances, and regional delicacies to their families in the United States.[40]

In August 1944, before he became married, George Eng and I received a three-day pass to Calcutta. The first thing we did after arriving was to find a place to spend the night. So we went to the USO building. We approached the information desk and asked the nice-looking, young white girl at the desk where we could find a clean and reasonable place to stay for two nights. To our delightful surprise she said, "You can stay at our house. There are two beds available. Twenty-five rupees a night for each one." We happily took her highly affordable offer.

It turned out that her father was a British major with a family of six. The next day Silvia invited two of her Indian girlfriends, who lived just across from her house, to go sightseeing with us. We visited Indian temples, window shopped at a local market, and had a nice lunch with the girls. It was definitely an event we, as young, single men away from our homes, remembered for a long time.

Around January 1945 our commanding officer Captain Victor S. Young, took on the additional duty as the USO officer. Company clerk Henry Chau and I learned how to set up a movie projector, screen, and loudspeaker, and how to thread the tape into the projector. They sent us two movies. We showed them to our headquarters group first.

Then, two days later, Henry and I packed all the equipment and took a twenty-minute train ride south to a Chinese Nationalist division headquarters to show them the movies. Movies could be shown only at night, so we had to stay a night at the division headquarters.

We came back to Kaiyuan the next day. Within a few days we would be off to another Chinese division headquarters, sometimes by road, to show the same movies. These land sojourns sometimes made us nervous; we were wary of the poor roads and primitive river crossings. Our superiors had warned us about the possibility of being attacked by thieves or bandits, but we never encountered any such incidents.

During these encounters with the Chinese soldiers, I realized that we shared much in common—language (to some degree), customs, beliefs, and importance of family ties—yet there was something that set us apart from them. They were Chinese, and we were Americans. Certainly both at the Kaiyuan headquarters and elsewhere we enjoyed many *ganbei* or "bottoms up" drinking parties with them where strong drink flowed freely, accompanied by good Chinese food in generous quantities. Some of us Americans, however, practiced "deceptive drinking," or managed moderation without giving insult. Undoubtedly the pressures of waging a war against a common enemy fostered such instances of camaraderie.

In the 987th Signal Company's table of organization, the company commander's rank is captain. For this officer there was no hope for further promotion within the unit. All of the team members were working in the field, and there was little for the captain to do. So he, Captain Young, requested for reassignment. In March his request was granted and he was assigned to OSS (Office of Strategic Service), with a promotion to major. That also ended our company's association with the USO.

However, Henry Chau and I were rewarded for this brief service with two weeks at the R&R (rest and recreation) camp that was a two-hour drive from Kaiyuan. On March 10, 1945, the two of us, thrilled by the prospect of enjoying the "good life" for a while, left the headquarters for two weeks of fun at the rest camp.

There was no bed check or roll call; what bliss. Each guest could sleep as late as he wished. The food was sensational and there was plenty of it. There was a huge lake with many rubber boats that we could paddle. There were shotguns we could check out to go hunting, which we did. However, there were few bushes or trees to harbor any kind of game. This was a plateau, just endless grassland. We came up to a small village and met some cheeky children and took pictures with them. We climbed into a water buffalo cart and rode to a Chinese army fort guarded by just two soldiers. One evening as we were about to start the movie, three Chinese generals and a middle-aged Chinese lady sat behind me. I turned around to take a look. I then realized that one of them was the Chinese defense minister. The entourage was on their way to the Southern Command front for an inspection tour. The R&R was a most pleasant diversion.

After Captain Young transferred out of the company, First Lieutenant William Ching took over as the company commander. May 8, 1945, marked V-E Day in Europe. The war was half won; "two down, one to go" became the name of our 21 Club. The government began the process of demobilization by devising a point system for determining which individual soldier was eligible to be discharged from the army. Lieutenant Ching had more than enough points to be eligible for immediate discharge. He left the company in early August 1945, before V-J Day, which was August 9. Second Lieutenant Thomas Hom was appointed the third company commander of the 987th Signal Company.

On August 6, 1945, the U.S. Air Force, using a B-29 bomber, dropped the first atomic bomb on Hiroshima, Japan. On August 9, 1945, the second atomic bomb fell on Nagasaki. On August 15, 1945, the emperor of Japan announced the acceptance of unconditional surrender.

On that V-J Day there was much merriment in the headquarters. At 21 Club things were getting rowdy. The men guzzled down bottles of cheap wine, bantered endlessly about their rosy futures, and grinned widely at each other. Philip Wong, the truck driver in the motor pool, kept urging me to drink mulberry wine with him, so much so that I got drunk. It was after midnight when I crawled back to my tent. When I lay down on my cot, the tent was revolving around my head. When I got up the next morning, I threw up and vomited out everything in my stomach. I really felt terrible and missed breakfast. Never again, I said to myself.[41]

On August 21, 1945, a delegation of five members of the Japanese general staff from Hanoi, French Indochina, arrived at the Southern Command headquarters at Kaiyuan to work out the surrender process with top-ranking Nationalist officers.[42] This was the only time I saw any Japanese during my service in China. To me, the Japanese, shorn of their uniforms, did not look any different from us. No wonder the Chinese were mistaken for "Japs" in the United States. The actual surrender of the Japanese troops in southern China took place in Hanoi.[43]

After the Japanese surrendered, the U.S. Army considered sending elements of our company into French Indochina to accompany the occupying American forces. Later, these orders were revised and the 987th personnel were withdrawn from the occupation forces.[44] The war officially ended on September 3, 1945.[45] Our company was ordered to return to the United States for deactivation on September 10, 1945. The men, myself included, were overjoyed. At last we were going home. We left Kaiyuan by train and arrived at Kunming on September 23, 1945. Here an incident occurred that gave the company its first experiences under gunfire.[46]

The men were quartered at Hostel 11d, which was flanked on one side by a compound of the Yunnanese provincial troops of General Lung Yun, and on the other by the compound of the Chinese Nationalist troops. On the morning of October 2, a power struggle–turned military conflict broke out between these two groups. The 987th men were caught in the path of the crossfire. During the day sporadic fire continued, though not of sufficient intensity to trigger undue alarm in our company. However, the stray bullets frequently were disconcertingly near, putting several holes in our tents.

Late in the evening the fire became extremely heavy, and one of the Chinese hostel workers was hit in the stomach, though not fatally. The camp commander then decided to evacuate. Each man grabbed a blanket or two and, under cover of darkness, moved to a comparatively safe area within a small courtyard beyond the Nationalist compound. Here we spent the rest of the night out in the open.

The tense situation of that night, however, forced the army to take precautions. In Kunming there was a large supply dump that a number of U.S. units relied on. It contained a large amount of gasoline, ordnance, clothing, food, and other supplies. Three roads led to that supply dump. The army feared that it might fall into the hands of the Yunnanese provincial troops or be ransacked during the confrontation. That night our company was ordered to take on roadblock guard duty. Teams of sixteen men each took turns guarding that dump. Everyone, including myself, carried a semiautomatic rifle. Each team was equipped with several .30 caliber machine guns. We stood guard until dawn. It was, however, a quiet night. By morning the Yunnan troops had surrendered, and we returned—our nerves somewhat frayed—to our formerly besieged hostel.

Meanwhile, during the previous hectic evening, one of our members, Bok Y. Gong, had traveled on a pass to Kunming. Because of the tumult, the U.S. military police picked Bok up and took him to the local USO for intensive questioning. They carefully checked his identification papers to make sure he was not an imposter. The authorities doubted he was an American soldier. They feared he was a Nationalist or Yunnan soldier who had stolen an American uniform along with the "dog tag." Bok spent a long restless night at the USO.

The next day the military police relayed the incident to the company commander and told him that it was fortunate Bok had on him his Chinese personal identification certificate (in Chinese), with photo affixed—a document issued to all U.S. soldiers in the CBI theater—that ascertained he was a member of the U.S. Army and denoted his rank. Otherwise Bok would have been subjected to greater scrutiny.

The normal strength of the 987th Signal Company was 123 men. For the convenience of personnel administration, 312 people were attached to our company, for a total of 435. Our entire company was airlifted back over the "Hump" to Calcutta on October 8, 1945.

We were billeted at the Hialeah race track. There was a nearby swimming pool. I was a good swimmer in high school, but after three years in the army I was somewhat below par in my endurance. Still, Harmon Woo and I decided to go for a vigorous swim.

I dived off a diving board and then tried to swim my way to the floating platform in the middle of a large swimming pool. I swam to within three feet of the floating platform when suddenly my legs cramped and my arms became overwhelmingly tired. I struggled to keep afloat and yelled for help. Three times I went down and came back up. Choking from all the water I had swallowed, I was gasping for air. I was certain then that there would be no fourth time. An American G.I. sitting on a floating platform saw what was transpiring. He dived headlong into the water and pulled me up, and then helped me to the platform. I rested for the next thirty minutes. The good Samaritan pointed out that the lifeguard—also an American G.I.—sitting up there in that high chair should have seen me struggling and rescued me. Since then I have always wondered why one person saved me and why another did not. I assume there were no racial overtones involved in the lifeguard's lack of response. This incident was a close call; I could have lost my life.

On November 11, 1945, we departed Calcutta on the SS *Marine Raven*, which took the Pacific route through the Malacca Straits to Manila, the Philippines, thence to Fort Lewis in Tacoma, Washington. We had been away from the United States for about eighteen long months. The company was deactivated on December 12, 1945.

I was given a traveling voucher to Fort Logan, Colorado, to complete the separation processing. A snowstorm in Billings, Montana, held us up for a day and a half. It was December 16 when we arrived at Fort Logan. On December 19, they handed me my uniform jacket, which was decorated with the three overseas service stripes, along with the Asiatic Pacific Service, World War II Victory, Good Conduct, Bronze Star, and China War Memorial medals. On December 21, 1945, they gave me my Honorable Discharge Certificate, the muster out pay, travel voucher back to Wichita, and all other discharge papers.[47] I returned to Wichita on December 22, 1945. It had been three years since I left.

Mar Sen Keol, the mother of Wayne Hung Wong (*far right*) holding sister Suit Wing, and brother Ying Kam (*far left*) in Guangdong, China, circa 1935. Courtesy of Wayne Hung Wong Collection.

Mar Tung Jing, alias Gee See Wing, and son Mar Ying Wing, alias Wayne Hung Wong, in Wichita, Kansas, circa 1936. Courtesy of Wayne Hung Wong Collection.

Wong Wing Lock, the "paper father" of Mar Ying Wing, alias Wayne Hung Wong, undated. Courtesy of Wayne Hung Wong Collection.

Wayne Hung Wong in his room above the Pan-American Café in Wichita, Kansas, circa 1936. Courtesy of Wayne Hung Wong Collection.

Pan-American Café, Wichita, Kansas, circa late 1930s. Courtesy of Wayne Hung Wong Collection.

Chinese male youngsters in Riverside Park area playing baseball in the 1930s, Wichita, Kansas, circa late 1930s. Courtesy of Wayne Hung Wong Collection.

Wayne Hung Wong at work in the Pan-American Café, Wichita, Kansas, circa early 1940s. Courtesy of Wayne Hung Wong Collection.

Students and teachers of Central Intermediate School, Wichita, Kansas, circa 1941. Wayne Hung Wong is in the fifth row from the front, third from the far left. Courtesy of Wayne Hung Wong Collection.

Chinese American youth including Wayne Hung Wong (*far left*) participating in a liberty bond parade in Wichita, Kansas, circa 1942. Courtesy of Wayne Hung Wong Collection.

Sergeant Wayne Hung Wong and fellow soldiers enjoying vacation in Wichita, Kansas, during World War II, circa 1943. Courtesy of Wayne Hung Wong Collection.

Wayne Hung Wong in his
uniform in Wichita, Kansas,
circa January 1946. Courtesy of
Wayne Hung Wong Collection.

Wedding of Wayne Hung Wong and Yee Kim Suey, Baisha, Taishan,
Guangdong, China, October 26, 1946. Courtesy of Wayne Hung Wong
Collection.

From left to right: sister Suit Wing, mother Sen Kell, wife Yee Kim Suey (*standing*), grandmother Soo Shee, brother Henjung (*seated on Soo Shee's lap*), Ying Wing (alias Wayne Hung Wong; *standing*), father Tung Jing, and brother Ying Kam (*standing*) in Baisha, Taishan, Guangdong, China, April 1947. Courtesy of Wayne Hung Wong Collection.

Wayne Hung Wong and Yee Kim Suey, Wichita, Kansas, circa 1947. Courtesy of Wayne Hung Wong Collection.

From left to right: Wilma, Edward, Wayne (*seated*), David, Kim Suey (*seated*), Linda, Wichita, Kansas, circa 1976. Courtesy of Wayne Hung Wong Collection.

美國第十四空軍（飛虎航空隊 ⬜⬜ 几八七特
第二次世界大戰期間在中緬 戰區服役同袍聯誼
五十五週年紀念 1942－1997
55TH ANNIVERSARY
HOME COMING OF THE C.B.I. FLYING TIGER 14TH AIR SERVICE GROUP &

Joint 55th anniversary celebration of the Fourteenth Air Service Group and 987th Signal Company, New York City, October 6–8, 1997. Courtesy of Wayne Hung Wong Collection.

CHAPTER 4

❦ ❦ ❦   Finding a War Bride

During the separation process, the lieutenant told me that I should enlist in the reserves for four years because of my rank as a staff sergeant. If there was a war I would retain my current rank; otherwise, I would have to start all over as a private. I would not be subjected to the call-up unless there was a war. Heeding that advice, I enlisted in the reserves for four years.[1]

My reserve enlistment expired on December 21, 1949. The authorities did send me the reenlistment form to fill out. By 1949 I was married and had two young children. So I returned the form and informed them I did not want to reenlist. As it turned out, the Korean War started in June 1950. With a wife who did not speak much English and two young children, it would have been a terrible struggle for them if I had gone off to Korea.

In July 1946 I learned that the passenger liner service between San Francisco and Hong Kong was available, after being interrupted since the start of the war period. I decided to return to China to see my father, mother, two brothers, and sister. I had not seen Mother and the siblings for more than ten years, and Father for about five. The separation had been far too long, particularly from my mother.

I left San Francisco in the last part of July 1946. The ship took twenty-eight days to reach Hong Kong. From Hong Kong it took an additional two days of travel by riverboat to get to the town of Sanbu, and from there I walked for two hours to Changlong, my parents' village. Rail transportation was nearly nonexistent since the Japanese during wartime had ripped the tracks out for their metal. When I reached the village it was already late August.

During the war Japan occupied Hong Kong, Guangzhou, and the large coastal cities. The rural areas were not damaged much, beyond a few buildings that were ransacked and fields that caught fire from sporadic bombings. Still, the desperate villagers needed money to buy food; the economy was in shambles and the currency worthless.[2] My parents' fate was a contrast to that of their peasant neighbors; they sold much of their jewelry to buy up a lot of land and hired people to farm it. They were living comfortably, though the pressure of living in the shadow of Japanese aggression seemed to have worn my mother down. She looked haggard and listless, seemingly nervous and uncertain.

After war's end my father was once again getting income from his real estate property in Hong Kong and Guangzhou. I went to Guangzhou to collect rent and to Hong Kong to claim stock dividends for him. I was really enjoying myself and having a good time becoming reacquainted with my family and relatives.

In the weeks after my return to Taishan, I resolved to find a wife. I was already twenty-four years old—already I was older than average for a man in China to first marry. I blamed my stay in the United States for this late entry into matrimony. In the past the Chinese Exclusion Act of 1882 prevented Chinese men from bringing their spouses to the United States. The GI Bill, however, gave me the right to bring my wife over.[3]

By then I had long determined that I was going to make my life in the United States; the sojourner status that my father and his partners envisioned for themselves was something I eschewed. It was not a real life. The separation from families, the lack of companionship, the loneliness—I had seen it all, and had no desire to be part of that contorted existence. Even if the circumstances prevented me from bringing a Chinese wife to the United States, I was still going to plant my roots in America. I would marry a local Chinese woman. Of course, World War II dramatically changed the circumstances, and probably staved off a family crisis.

In my village an exciting buzz about the monumental changes in U.S. immigration laws went around. Suddenly relatives, friends, and neighbors took note of their young female villagers, reminding them that *Gum Saan* was now within reach. A matchmaker—a haggard old lady—visited with my mother and clucked about the virtues of a number of the potential daughters-in-law. All of them were supposedly ravishing beauties—demure, soft-spoken, and dutiful daughters. My mother, eager to have her eldest son married off before the other off-spring—a traditional concern of Chinese parents—pressed the names onto me.

I, though equally eager to meet the women, did harbor some ambivalent feelings. After all, I was picking a wife in a hurry with the assistance of a woman who knew little of my wants, desires, and needs. Eventually my desire for a family overcame my doubts. I met twelve avid women—short, tall, thin, overweight—before I met Yee Kim Suey in the middle of September 1946.

My first encounter with Kim took place in her parents' home in the Daixing village, not too far from my parents. She was a seventeen-year-old girl with a pear-shaped face and large, pearl-like eyes, along with a well-formed nose that ended in thick lips. I was smitten, but barely said a word to her. Kim was equally quiet; she greeted me and my parents, and then disappeared.

Meanwhile my parents and her parents had been, with the help of the matchmaker, comparing the genealogical and horoscopic data on Kim and me. They made sure we were indeed a marriage made in heaven, one the Gods had predetermined as a suitable match. Once that ritual was over, they conferred on the elaborate arrangements for the impending engagement, which included the exchange of rings and gifts of pastries, cakes, and chicken for the bride's family. Our families went ahead and arranged for the time and date of the marriage, which was set for October 26, 1946.[4]

On the night before the wedding, Kim, surrounded by female relatives, had her hair combed and "put up." This represented her symbolic initiation into domestic life. I for my part was "capped," which meant that I was ready for the responsibilities of marriage.

On that day we were married according to the traditional Chinese customs. My family went to the bride's family house and brought with them a munificent dowry that included money, pastries, dumplings, fruit, sets of silk clothing for the bride and her parents, and other gifts for Kim's family. Kim then was carried by hired men in a swaying sedan chair draped in red silk cloth from her village to mine, but in a circuitous route. When her sedan chair arrived outside my parents' house, I approached it with much confidence and invited her to leave the chair and enter the festooned house. This traditional ritual symbolized her entry into my family and the leaving behind of the ties to her natal family. The ceremony concluded with prayers and the burning of joss sticks at the family altar. Following that, Kim and I served cups of tea to the older relatives—which symbolized the betrothed couple's respect for the elders—and in return the relatives handed us gifts of money and jewelry. The day ended with a big, joyous feast of multiple courses of shark fin soup, suckling pig, salted stir-fried shrimp, and other delectable dishes. Several days later Kim and I visited her parents in their house.[5]

We went to Guangzhou and Hong Kong for a month-long honeymoon. From the start, I intended to bring Kim back to the United States as a war bride. Because the United States government did not recognize a Chinese civil marriage, we had to go through a Christian marriage.[6] Along with two other Chinese GIs and their new wives, all six of us arranged with the U.S. Consulate Office at Guangzhou to have the Christian wedding at that office on January 3, 1947. My second marriage ceremony was certified by Calvin Lee, an ordained Christian minister, and it was witnessed by the Vice Consul Harold G. McConeghey.

In April 1947 we were on our way to the United States on a passenger liner, the *General Gordon*.[7] After we were married I intensively coached Kim about my "paper son" background, including the "fact" that that my surname was Wong, not Mar. I told her all about my paper family members. For example, I reminded her: "Look, I have five brothers, you know, and not just two brothers and no sisters. There are no daughters in our family, since all five are sons." I drilled into her the name of the village and the layout of the houses, the location of the family house, outhouse, and water well, the placement of the furniture, where each member of the paper family slept, and anything else I could think of to prepare her for the grueling immigration proceedings.

At that moment I no longer had the precious deposition book in my hands. Without it I had to rely on my memory, hoping it would not fail me in this crucial time. I anticipated that Kim could be detained if her deposition did not match what was in my file, and I was determined to avoid that fate. Kim was quiet throughout these "coaching" sessions; she did look pensive during those times.

We came back to the United States in luxurious first-class accommodations. The trip from Hong Kong to San Francisco lasted about twenty-eight days. Twelve days into the trip the immigration officer began processing the immigration papers—such a preliminary processing was absent when I first came to the United States in 1935. He started with the first-class section. I estimated that there were about 350 Chinese nationals onboard the ship. I was the eleventh person he interviewed. He checked my passport, the army discharge paper, the immunization record, and the marriage certificate issued by the U.S. consulate office. Everything was in order.

Both of us were present during the interview. The immigration inspector asked me a series of questions. I think he wanted to make sure that I was indeed the husband of Kim and that Kim was not entering the country under false pretenses. He asked about my particulars, Kim's biographical background, and the date of our marriage. He also queried me about the names of my brothers, and their present whereabouts. I had to also show my marriage certificate, the Chinese certificate of identity, honorable discharge certificate, and U.S. passport.[8] My wife came with me as a war bride of a U.S. veteran, which was a perfectly legitimate entry, I reminded myself, even as I nervously wondered about clearing the later hurdle in San Francisco.

After our interview, the officer, Stanley, whose last name I am unable to remember, asked me, "Mr. Wong, would you care to be my interpreter?" I replied, "I'd be more than happy to do it." I think he asked me because, unlike my father or many of his peers, I had the good fortune to receive an education in the United States. As such, he probably felt that I was competent enough to play the role of interpreter.

Every day we worked for a good number of hours. Stanley put every passenger through the same drill: he checked their documents, which could include their U.S. certificate of identity that attested they were permanent residents of the United States, health records, passports, and army discharge papers in the case of veterans. He posed questions to the passengers, mostly to verify that the information in the documents was up-to-date and accurate. Stanley was never confrontational. In some way, I found the whole process rather perfunctory; I suppose the more rigorous process was yet to come. About four days before we docked at San Francisco we had processed all the potential new arrivals.

En route to California we stopped in Honolulu, Hawaii, for two days. Politely I asked Stanley if it were possible for us to go on shore for a day, citing our dislike of being cooped up for the last twenty-some days. He readily gave his consent and handed us a pass for a one-night stay. We hired a taxi cab and the driver took us for a spin all the way around the island and then into Honolulu. We partook of a delicious Chinese dinner there, spent a night in a dingy budget motel, and the next morning headed back to the ship for the last stretch to the United States.

We docked at San Francisco on May 3, 1947. The ones with a U.S. passport cleared immigration processing unencumbered. However, all of the war brides, young and old alike, were bused to the four- to five-story immigration building in San Francisco for processing, even though they were perfectly legitimate immigrants.[9]

During the processing on the ship, we had to inform the authorities where we would stay so that they could get in touch with me. Onboard the ship a list of hotels was made available to all immigrants, so I chose the Pickwick Hotel in downtown San Francisco. I checked into that hotel, and waited.

The wait was nerve-wracking; not knowing what Kim was undergoing troubled me. Sleep eluded me; my mind wandered to the early years of journeying to the United States, the endless labor, the adventures of wartime service, and my recent festive marriage.

Three long days had passed since Kim was detained. On the third day, the authorities finally telephoned me at the hotel and asked me to come down to the immigration office to pick up Kim. I was elated. My wife was the first to get out of the detention building. She did not look worn out or weary.

Excitedly, on the way back to the hotel, I asked Kim what kind of questions the officers had posed to her. She said she was the first person to be interrogated and that they did not ask her too many questions. The officers queried about my paper family structure, such as the names of the paper father, mother, and the five brothers, as well as the name

of the village. Then there were several other questions about the location of the chicken coop, the outdoor house, and where I slept in the
house. Her interrogation apparently was an extraordinarily short one,
and I attribute the rapid processing and Kim's release to my role as an
interpreter for the immigration authorities.[10]

Kim estimated that there were about 180 to 200 war brides detained
in that building. She said there were a lot of internees who had been
there for as long as two or three months. Some women were pregnant,
while others were contemplating suicide. A number of the women were
emotionally distraught, and a few were crying constantly.[11]

By August 1947 the situation in the detention building was dete-
riorating. The backlog of war bride cases had doubled, the tension in
that building was mounting, and a solution was nowhere in sight. The
Chinese community in San Francisco turned to Congress for redress.
They wanted to know why white American veterans who brought their
war brides into the United States gained immediate admission, while
Chinese veteran war brides had to go through detention and interrogation. Chinese Americans cried foul; they called the process unfair and a
form of discrimination. Because Chinese American veterans had been
willing to sacrifice their lives to fight for their country, and as such had
laid claim to their birthright, they too should be treated in the same
way as the Caucasians. By order of Congress the unequal treatment of
Chinese war brides was stopped. Most of the war brides in our ship
spent six or seven days in the detention building. Thereafter all war
brides were admitted freely.[12]

My paper brother, Hung Doon, returned to China in April 1947. I
was on my way with my war bride to the United States while he was
en route to China. He was drafted into the U.S. Army in September
1941, just before the Pearl Harbor attack, and had served in the South
Pacific theater for almost four years. Hung Doon returned to the United
States sometime in 1948. He brought his wife of more than twenty years
with him, and his number one "son," Gin Kin, who was at that time
eighteen years old.[13]

In truth, Hung Doon had no children of his own. He sold both of his
paper sons' slots to several eager buyers before he returned to China.
At the last minute, just before Hung Doon left China, the buyer of

the number two son's slot changed his mind. Therefore Hung Doon brought in just one son and told the immigration officials that his number two "son" wished to stay in China with his grandmother and that he might want to come to the United States later. As far as I know, no one ever came over as his number two "son."

United States immigration officials have always known that all Chinese immigration papers were irregular; one way or the other, something was amiss. The most telltale sign was that every offspring that a Chinese immigrant registered was a son. No one chose to register a daughter at all. They figured that once their daughter was married, she belonged to the other family. Because she could not carry the family name, there was no reason to bring her into the United States. There was always a heavy demand for paper sons, but no demand for paper daughters.[14]

I believe everything came to a head around 1960. Congress passed a law to make it possible for all Chinese to come forward to confess their true identity and straighten the records of their contorted immigration histories.[15] Sometime in 1962 Gin Kin, Hung Doon's number one paper son, wished to sponsor the immigration of his birth parents to the United States. To that end, he had to confess to the authorities his falsified identity, thus implicating everyone in my extended paper family.

In April 1964 the immigration services duly notified me what had happened and urged me to correct my papers. Initially I was worried. I had not confessed thus far because I harbored fears of the unknown. To me, confessing had an obvious impact: my citizenship status would be jeopardized. Now, however, I had no choice—the "game" was up. Kim and I were told to appear for an interview at the local courthouse on Third and Market Streets. I filled out a set of forms that queried my "true" and "paper" family roots as well as the current whereabouts of all family members, in turn forcing me to implicate other relatives. I admitted to my fraudulent claim of citizenship, and denied ever having committed any criminal acts, belonging to the Communist Party, or believing in communism. I also turned over my passport and certificate of identity.[16] At the interview, I learned that by being a veteran I would not have to suffer through the long waiting period mandated before a paper son could reclaim his U.S. citizenship. In fact, I could have driven up to Kansas City the next week and undergone the naturalization. Instead, owing to work commitments, I chose to wait for about five weeks for the next immigration swearing-in session at a local court on August 31, 1964.

As for Kim Suey, she had just gone through naturalization in May 1963, but using my paper identity. She had waited all this time—sixteen years to be exact—before taking this step. The delay stemmed from her poor English skills. Finally, her desire to sponsor her brothers—who had earlier fled to Hong Kong during the early years of the Communist regime—to immigrate to the United States pushed her to more aggressively learn the language. She was willing to endure the countless drills I put her through. However, all that effort came to naught when officials voided her naturalization papers as improper, and she had to wait five more years to get back her naturalized status on May 7, 1968.[17] Soon after that, she did sponsor the immigration of her brothers and they came to America in either 1969 or 1970.[18]

During my naturalization proceedings in 1964, I could have reclaimed my true surname, Mar. I knew that a lot of other Chinese who went through the confession program did choose to do so. I suppose they wished to clarify their family genealogy and pass on rectified personal histories to subsequent generations. However, my army record, property titles, insurance record, the children's names on their birth certificates, and their school records were all in the name of Wong. I did not want to go through all those changes and explanations for why I had to change my name, so I kept Wong. I was also particularly worried that I would face complications later if I had to access veterans' benefits, such as using the veterans' hospital.[19] However, all of my children have Mar as their middle name, and this was a way for them to know their true name. When the children grew up, I told them the truth; none of them reacted negatively to the revelation.

CHAPTER 5

❦ ❦ ❦   Raising a Family in Wichita

After Kim was released from the detention building, we stayed in San Francisco for two more days. We then headed for Wichita by train. I think it was about June 15, 1947, when we arrived in Wichita. It had been five long years since I left North High School. The wartime economy was scaling back—assembly lines stopped running, people moved back to the countryside, and the inflation rate was climbing. All or most of the defense work had disappeared.[1]

My first encounter with racial discrimination might have been when I brought my bride from China to Wichita in June 1947. We tried for the next two months to find an apartment or house to live in within walking distance of the restaurant where I worked. We scoured the newspapers for vacancies of apartments, houses, even rooms to rent. Every day we trudged the sidewalks and streets. Summer always arrives early in Kansas—soaked with perspiration, and legs wearied, we ambled on.

Everywhere we went we were told there was no vacancy. We never encountered any landlord who was rude or said anything that upset us. Without a doubt, however, we were told politely over and over again that we had to look elsewhere. One landlady, an elderly woman with a seemingly sweet disposition, said, "I am so sorry. The apartment was just taken." Was it really true there was no vacancy, or just a mere "coincidence"? Having resigned ourselves to the reality, we turned to boarding in a hotel and went to the restaurant for our meals.[2]

Now that I was married and shouldered new responsibilities, my work at my father's restaurant became a noticeably time-consuming effort. By then my father had returned from China, but not without facing an unexpected problem. Earlier, before leaving for China in 1941, he had filed some income tax forms using "Gee" as his paper surname. However, when he tried to secure a visa in 1948 at the U.S. consulate in Hong Kong, the authorities told him that his immigration records—which entered his surname as "Jee"—did not square with that income tax paper trail. Denied a visa, he wrote to me for help. I had to scramble and send additional documents such as family photographs and other evidence that showed he was indeed who he said he was. I even contacted a local newspaper reporter who wrote an article about my father's plight, and sent that off to the authorities.[3] Finally the authorities did relent and issue a visa, but not after some months had passed since the initial application.

Far less fortunate was my second brother, Ying Kam. He bought the slot of the son of Mar Sui Fong, the latter being the son of my father's cousin, Henry Mar. Having assumed the identity of Sui Fong's son, Ying Kam applied to immigrate in 1947. When he appeared at the U.S. consulate office in Hong Kong for the interrogation, his testimony did not corroborate with that of Sui Fong. Ying Kam never came to the United States.

With a baby on the way, in March 1948 we bought our first house—a two-bedroom bungalow—at 944 South Market for $5,000, with $1,000 down and at 6 percent annual interest.[4] Our first child, Linda, was born on May 1, 1948. Our second child, David, was born on May 23, 1949. The third child, Wilma, was born on May 29, 1950.

The period between 1947 and 1949 was hard for my family. I toiled for twelve-hour days six days a week, and made about $240 a month as the night chef at the Pan-American Café. The pay left very little money to save for future investments. We could not afford even a secondhand car during those years. When I got off work in the morning, I walked the nine long blocks from the restaurant to my house to avoid the five cents bus fare. I bought milk from the restaurant's milkman at wholesale price, which was three cents per quart cheaper than at the grocery store. So by walking home and carrying two quarts of milk, I saved eleven cents a day for two or three years. I also salvaged the empty flour sacks from the restaurant for my wife to sew infant clothing for the three children. Scoured pots and pans, dulled knives and forks, and chipped china that the restaurant no longer had any use for became our kitchenware. We made do without an easy chair or sofa. The only things we bought—and on ninety-day credit—were the bed, stove, refrigerator, and dining room table and chairs.

There was an established, though rundown, poultry house about three blocks from our house. Every day the workers disposed of chicken feet that no white people would ever eat. Once a week I walked over and filled a bucket with chicken feet and then stewed them with peanuts and scallions as dinner. Later, when I worked at a supper club, I went to the nearby slaughterhouse and picked up free beef kidney, ox tails, and entrails and made meals out of them. Those were hard times for us. Throughout these years Kim never complained; sometimes, however, the pressure did get to her. She bemoaned that her family was so far away.

The sluggish economy improved again during the Korean War. With the war raging from 1950 onward, the Boeing company's production line revved up. Boeing developed a new bomber called the B-47 and began building new units of it, followed by units of the inimitable B-52.[5] During the Korean War, business thrived at the Pan-American Café and we made a little more money. In September 1952 we bought the two duplexes at 1202 South St. Francis for $12,000 with $3,000 down. This was the start of my investment in real estate—an entrepreneurial activity I learned from my father's business dealings in Guangzhou and Hong Kong.

In the 1950s I did not encounter discrimination in buying real estate for investment purposes. However, I knew that in College Hill they had a neighborhood association, which bound homeowners to sell properties only to white Americans.[6] I never had the resources to buy a house in College Hill, so that exclusion never gave me any torment. If people did not want me there, then neither did I wish to live there. With the little money we had, we were lucky to buy any house in any neighborhood. We never had a problem buying properties anywhere else, although in the early years I concentrated on buying properties that were close to the family house so that it would be easier to care for them.

Because I had enlisted in the Army before finishing high school, I now took a GED test and passed it. I went to night school to earn my

American History credit in April 1952, and received my North High School diploma in May 1952.[7]

Our children were growing up, and so did the cost of our household. In the middle of April 1953, Albert Mar, owner of Albert's Restaurant, a Chinese American establishment, called me at home.

He said, "Wayne, would you like to work for me at my restaurant for $325 a month? The hours are from 10:00 A.M. to 10:00 P.M. The restaurant is closed on Tuesday."

"Yes," I replied.

"You can start work on May 1," Albert explained.

At the Pan-American Café I was being paid $280 a month. I left my father's restaurant—much to my father's consternation—for more money.

Yet just two and a half years later I developed doubts about that decision. The darkest day in my life was the last Monday in November 1955. Just three days before Thanksgiving, Albert called me at around 10:30 P.M. just after I had arrived home from work. He gruffly said, "Wayne, you don't need to come to work anymore." He then abruptly hung up.

With three children to support and a fourth child, Edward, on the way, I was a little worried. However, despite losing that job, we were not in a desperate situation. Our rental income from our two duplexes gave us some cushion in these difficult times.

To this day I still do not know why I was fired. The only reason I can think of are a set of circumstances related to an incident in the middle of September 1955. One day at around noon I received a call at work from a hysterical Kim. Between sobs, an incoherent Kim relayed that six-year-old David was a victim of an accident. I told Albert, the restaurant manager, that I had to leave. Albert, without hesitation, snapped, "You can't go in this busy lunch hour." I calmly but firmly replied, "My boy got hit by a car; I must go home to see what I can do to help him." Hastily, I took off my apron and dashed home, over his objection.

When I arrived home Kim told me she had gone to school to bring David home for lunch. David and his friend Tse Chien were running home on Market Street. About three houses before reaching home,

David was running across the street at Market and Gilbert Streets. Suddenly a fast-moving automobile appeared from nowhere and hit David. The police came and a report was filed. The driver was charged for running a stop sign.

I examined David and did not see any visible cuts or bruises. He was shaken and was crying in pain. Within the hour David was urinating blood. So I called Dr. MacLeod, our family doctor, and told him what had happened. He instructed me to take David immediately to St. Francis Hospital.

At the hospital David was in critical condition. The doctor said he was suffering from internal bleeding and that one of his kidneys was badly bruised. For the next three days we waited for David to rally while the hemorrhaging continued. At the start of the third day of the ordeal, Dr. MacLeod said that if the bleeding did not stop on that day, then surgery was necessary to carry out a procedure to stop the hemorrhaging. Fortunately at 5:00 P.M. the doctor called me at work and said that David was fine since the bleeding had stopped. If my defiance of Albert's objection had resulted in my dismissal, then I have no regrets.

After that stint at Albert's, I spent a few months at the Red Barn Restaurant as a cook. In April 1956 I saw an advertisement in the "help wanted" column of a local newspaper for a kitchen manager at the T-Bone Supper Club on 47th Street South and Broadway. The club featured a nightly sophisticated burlesque show. I went there to put in my application. The next day Mr. Kenneth Tague called me to come in for an interview. I was hired and started working the same evening; my pay was $125 per week. For the next sixteen years I stayed there as the kitchen manager-cum-cook, offering patrons a variety of steak and seafood dishes.[8] I hired all of the kitchen staff, which included two black short-order cooks and a black dishwasher—all of them were reliable people.

The T-Bone was a busy establishment; customers typically were businesspeople who dropped in for regular go-go girl shows at 8:00, 9:00, and 10:00 P.M. The girls—typically voluptuous and leggy—were always clothed; the law required them to wear at least a g-string, and to cover their breasts. To increase the level of titillation, the girls wore pasties. Bringing their own liquor, because the local laws prohibited such clubs from serving it, the customers threw a lot of money around but were always orderly.[9] Not so at the Blu Note Ballroom on 31st Street near the Boeing plant. Also owned and run by Kenny, it had an infamous reputation for showing "lewd" or pornographic films and offering all types of gambling games. Brawls often broke out. The club was raided a number of times, and eventually Kenny was found guilty of running illegal gambling games and sentenced to jail for one year.[10]

Our fourth child, Edward, was born on May 18, 1956. Space was running out at the Market Street dwelling. In 1957 we bought our second house, with three bedrooms, at 1020 South Water. We put in a 20 ft. x 25 ft. basement. We also put in central heating and a new water heater in the basement. We installed hardwood flooring in all rooms except the kitchen. We rented out the old house for two years and then sold it. I also invested my money in good stocks and bonds. Then in 1961 we bought an all-brick fourplex at 2322 East Harry Street. The year before Linda graduated from high school, which was 1966, we bought a nine-unit brick apartment at 1801 East English.

In the early years of our marriage, Kim took care of the children and the household chores, while I slaved at the club during the evenings and in the daytime took care of the rental properties. Kim, however, initially knew only the basics of preparing Chinese food. She was a young girl of seventeen years when she married me, and had depended on her parents for all of those years, although her mother did expose her a little to cooking. Because I had been cooking since my teenage years, I taught her how to prepare the time-consuming Chinese roast duck. Because there was not a Chinese grocery store or Chinese bakery in Wichita, Kim, picking up tips from Chinese female friends in town, eventually learned to make from scratch delicate pastries, tasty cakes, and other delicious dishes.

When the children were growing up, Kim and I wanted both the girls and boys to have the best possible education. We raised them believing that, regardless of their sex, they should strive to achieve the most in life. We also believed in Chinese traditions; we instilled in them the need to respect their elders as well as the intrinsic value of being mindful of one's responsibilities. Kim and I emphasized education throughout their schooling. We expected them to go to school, return home, study, do their chores, and go to sleep. This sounds harsh, but we truly wanted them to succeed and fulfill their ambitions. Our hope was that they would never have to struggle the way we did.

When Linda was in high school, David and Wilma in junior high, and Edward still in elementary school, we had this old black and white television, console style. By then Kim had gone to work at the T-Bone club as a dishwasher. She had grown weary of playing the role of housewife. She was tired of being cooped up in the house with four energetic children. We agreed that the children could be left to their own devices. In those days, both Kim and I worked nights. Kim cooked dinner in the late afternoons, so the children would be fed before we left for work. The children were left on their own to do their homework. We soon discovered, however, that was not the case; they were watching far too much television at night and falling behind in their homework. Therefore, every evening before Kim went to work, she would pull the picture tube out of the television, forcing the children to do their studies. She realized there was a problem and she fixed it.

Kim had more influence on the children because she was at home far more than I. She taught the girls—Linda and Wilma—to hang the wash on a clothesline. They learned how to starch and iron clothes. The girls were given bathroom duties such as scouring the sink and mopping the floors on a weekly basis. Because money was tight in the 1950s, the children and Kim walked to the grocery stores, and the girls helped Kim carry the groceries. They often shopped at several stores to get the best deals. They walked over to Farha Brothers on Water and Douglas Streets, then to the nearby Thriftway, then to Dillons and Safeway, all of which were within a radius of several miles. Without even a wagon, the children and their mother carried the groceries by hand, even during snowy days. Linda and Wilma also took care of their younger male siblings; they walked them to school and back to the house. Kim expected far less from the boys in terms of chores; she probably spoiled them a little.

I taught the children, particularly the boys, the critical importance of saving money and investing it wisely. When the children were still rather young, I placed their money in individual savings accounts. When Edward was five years old and still in kindergarten, I picked him up one afternoon from school and took him down to meet my stockbroker at Payne Webber. He helped Edward invest some of the money I had saved for him from past birthdays and Christmas celebrations in ten shares of stocks. My parting shot to Edward on that day: "Make your money work for you." It was advice I imparted to all of the children.

The children—both the boys and girls—had to contribute to the upkeep of the rental properties. All of them had to pitch in and help out. The children took turns mowing the lawn. Whenever a tenant moved out, they mopped and waxed the floors, vacuumed carpeted areas, scrubbed the toilets, painted the walls, wiped down the kitchen counters, cleaned appliances such as the refrigerator and stove, and did any other general maintenance work.[11]

I recruited Linda and Wilma to work at the T-Bone Supper Club, mostly for the busy weekends. When they became older teenagers, they washed dishes, trimmed and cut vegetables, and took out the garbage. Linda was the "salad girl"—the one who replenished the salad bar—while Wilma grew into the role of prep cook. They worked evening hours—from seven until two in the morning; by the time they cleaned up the kitchen it was almost 4:00 A.M. Later David and Edward also came to help. One memory I have was that Edward, as an eight year old, rolled bacon around fillets of meat; being so short and small he had to stand on a stack of boxes to reach the kitchen counters. Both boys worked as dishwashers. David eventually became a bartender at the club. The children did receive wages for the work they did at the T-Bone.

The children learned to speak Chinese at home. Kim spoke Chinese to them. But they never had the opportunity to know how to read and write the language. Unlike the Chinese in San Francisco or some other large cities, the Chinese community in Wichita was small and fragmented. There were about thirty such families in the city in the 1950s. So Wichita never had a Chinese-language school in that era.

Before the children started schooling, they learned very little English at home. Kim spoke hardly any of this language until she went to work in the outside world, and that did not happen until the girls were in high school and old enough to care for their siblings. When Linda, the oldest, went off to kindergarten, her teacher one day asked me to drop by the school.

After exchanging some pleasantries, this young, enthusiastic teacher said in a slightly exasperated tone: "Mr. Wong, I couldn't make her understand me at all. I understand she doesn't speak very much English."

"Well, I understand that, that's why I'm sending her to school, she doesn't speak English," I said matter-of-factly.

After Linda went to school, she was able to start teaching her siblings some English. Without any preschool in the 1950s, my children learned little of it until they started school.

They did pick up some basic English when a female missionary, Mary Adams, came to our house to proselytize. Adams was a dedicated missionary who witnessed to many Chinese "heathens," both old and young, in Wichita. Apparently she had served a stint in China, and believed that her mission could continue in Wichita. Every Saturday she came to the house, starting when Linda was only four years old and continuing until my daughter turned nineteen. Ms. Adams taught Bible verses and stories using cut-out pictures of biblical characters on felt cloth.

Wilma, Linda, and David also received biblical lessons during their grade school years at the Lincoln School on Lincoln and Topeka. An hour of each weekday was set aside to attend a church near the school. The children attended in various grades the Grace Methodist Church, the Broadway Christian Church, and the First Church of God. One day the minister from the First Church of God on Market and Lincoln Streets, the Reverend E. E. Kardazke, came to our house and introduced himself. He urged me to let the children attend the church, and I readily assented. They went to that church all the way until they were in high school. My wife and I did not attend church, although we did celebrate Christmas and believed in God.

During their elementary school days, Linda and Wilma interacted with the white children in the neighborhood. They skated, biked, rode go-carts, and played jacks, cards, and board games. They wanted to join the BlueBirds and the Camp Fire Girls but never did because we did not have spare money for the various activities and uniforms. They were avid readers who went regularly to the Wichita public library, and came home with stacks of books.[12]

Social life for the girls became more segregated as they grew older. As older teenagers, Wilma and Linda joined some neighborhood Chinese youngsters and every summer they drove off to Nederland, Colorado, for an annual retreat at their Sunday school teacher's cabin. They hung out with a group of local Chinese youth. I remember that the girls of that group, Wilma included, wore bell-bottoms and loud, colored shirts with leather tie strings with eyelets. They came over to our house at 1020 South Water. They danced in the basement, and played 45 RPMs to the music of Dick Clark's *Bandstand* and that wild British band, the Beatles.[13]

During high school they interacted very little with the students of West High School. Wilma, for example, wanted to join the West High Pep Club, but again we did not have the spare money for the uniform. Wilma was quite disappointed when we barred her from attending both her junior- and senior-year proms, especially because for at least one of them, a popular football letterman invited her to the dance. Years later we found out that at church activities, Linda and Wilma met servicemen from McConnell Air Force Base and dated them behind our backs. We were disappointed with them.[14]

Kim and I were wary of the boys and girls dating outside of the Chinese culture; we were afraid that they would be hurt by the larger society. We also wanted to preserve the Chinese culture in our family. Therefore we disapproved of them dating, let alone marrying non-Chinese. As time passed, and as we grew older, Kim and I realized that times had changed and that as long as they, the children, were satisfied with whom they picked, then we were content with the situation. We also realized that this is a multicultural society; with few Chinese to date in Wichita, we had to accept the idea of interracial marriage.[15] Both David and Edward, however, did marry Chinese women. Wilma married a Chinese man, but like Edward's marriage, hers ended in divorce. Linda, however, never married.

Even in the 1960s the children continued to be largely excluded from extracurricular activities. Edward felt different in school because we still did not have the money then to give him well-tailored clothing or allow him to participate in school events. He felt conspicuous during the height of the Vietnam War. A lot of the students were unfriendly to him, not knowing he was Chinese rather than Vietnamese. In school they sometimes called him a "gook." I think he did hurt a lot in those days. When he came to complain to me, I told him: "You have to accept people for how they are; whether they like you or not, you still have to treat them with respect and kindness."[16]

The children did develop a few friendships with white peers. Their few white friends—more Edward's than the other older siblings'—were interested in the cultural differences between Chinese and white America. They were intrigued by Chinese New Year rituals such as the handing out of little red envelopes that contained money for good luck. They found our food "exotic"—chicken feet, cow brains, and beef tongue are not exactly common fare in American households.

The children met a few more white Americans through their involvement in church community fund-raising activities, the most popular one being an annual paper drive where they raised forty cents for every one hundred pounds of newspapers. They also handed out food baskets to the underprivileged. Kim and I encouraged their involvement in these activities, trusting that they molded the children to be empathetic to the less fortunate. Besides, these were supervised activities, so we were not worried about the people they hung out with.

Every Independence Day the small Chinese community in Wichita gathered for a memorable picnic at Riverside Park. It was the one day a year when Chinese business owners in town took the day off. The children went swimming in the Arkansas River, then unpolluted; played hide-and-seek around the bushes and trees; and fed the animals at the park's zoo. The older youngsters sometimes played baseball or board games. Under these shady trees, the adults set up collapsible card tables, and played mahjong for small bets. The women gossiped about their children and their families in China and the United States; the men exchanged stories about their growing businesses. Each family brought home-cooked food for the picnic. Kim prepared delicious barbecued pork-fried rice, while other women fixed delicious crispy fried chicken, chow mein, fruit salad, and shrimp cocktail.

When all the food had been consumed, and all appetites satiated, the conversation sometimes turned serious. By then we knew all about the Communist regime in China. The Communists are godless people.

They tried to destroy the Chinese tradition, one that was centered on ancestral worship and performing good deeds. They forced the villagers in Taishan to tear down the memorial buildings and destroy ancestral tablets. They then promised all the tenant farmers ownership of the land, but instead the land fell into the hands of the government. During the 1950s and 1960s we received letters from our clanspeople complaining of the heavy taxation, famines, and droughts. The subsistence of the families was reduced to grass and tree roots. Starvation stalked the countryside.

For my mother and my youngest brother, Henjung, life in Changlong was fraught with tension, even turning bloody at times. The Communists targeted my family because we were considered part of the hated landowner class. Periodically the local Communist cadres would haul my mother and Henjung away from the house and force her to kneel on broken glass in the center of the village. Neighbors, friends, and relatives were ordered to encircle her. Then the heckling began. The soldiers called Mother a "traitor," "capitalist," and other epithets. They kicked her and beat her until blood trickled down from her face, arms, and knees. Quite often she was in so much pain that she could not even crawl home. With her knees injured, she sat on the ground, and with the help of her arms, pushed her posterior forward. This was how she finally got home.[17]

In 1952 the Chinese Communist government gave Mother the option of divesting herself of all family-owned properties in exchange for permission to leave for Hong Kong to join her relatives there. Mother accepted the offer, and she, Ying Kam, and Henjung moved to Hong Kong and lived there until 1959. In that year, the Catholic Relief Services offered to bring refugees such as my mother and Henjung to the United States. My father and I sent them a check for $2,000 to cover the required expenses, including the air tickets. Mother was reluctant to leave China, but she did so for the sake of Henjung so that he could have a better education and life. By then, Ying Kam had raised a family of his own in Hong Kong and had no desire to move to a foreign land. My sister, Suit Wing, was still in Guangzhou, practicing as a Western-trained physician. She eventually left for Hong Kong in 1972.

When Mother settled in Wichita, life did not get any easier for her.

Often at night she had nightmares. She kept mumbling in her sleep, "the Communists are coming for me." Fearful of the past, she would leave the house at night and wander around in the neighborhood. When Henjung married in 1970, this woman, with hardly any English skills and already well past eighty years old, on a daily basis left the house to catch a public bus to his house to spend the night. The next morning she would take the bus to return home. Such was her routine for years to come until she passed away.

There was not much I could do about that situation. During my years at the T-Bone Club I went to work at about 4:00 P.M. and rarely came home until 1:00 in the morning. While the children were awake, I was asleep. Sundays were the only days on which I spent any leisure time with my own family. I took the family to the popular A&W Restaurant and we enjoyed hamburgers, french fries, and root beer floats. Later in the afternoons I took the children swimming and the boys fishing in the Arkansas River.

In 1967—the year David graduated from West High School—the family made its highly anticipated three-week-long vacation. We rented a new four-door Dodge and left at the crack of dawn. David, Wilma, and I shared the driving. Our lunch stop was at a Chinese friend's restaurant in Liberal, Kansas. We spent the night in the quaint town of Tucumcari, New Mexico. The next day we had lunch at Flagstaff, Arizona. We spent the night in sprawling Phoenix, Arizona, visiting with my uncle and aunt's family. This aunt was the first daughter of my grandfather. It was an emotional and happy reunion after twenty years of separation, since the last time I saw them in China was just after the war.

The next day we arrived in Anaheim, California. We bought all-day tickets for fun-filled Disneyland. In the evening I called an old Chinese friend in Los Angeles. He said he would be happy to show us the town. The following day, after the tour of L.A., we drove down to San Diego and then onward to Tijuana, Mexico. We shopped in Tijuana, and then returned to San Diego to spend the night. The next day we headed north on Highway 5. Our first stop was Stockton, California, to see an old friend and her family from our village in China. It had been twenty years since we had seen each other.

After dinner we continued on our way to see my cousin William D. Marjo and his family in Redding, California, where he was operating two restaurants. It had been thirty long years since I last saw him. We sure had a lot to catch up on. Before I went to bed I called an old army buddy, Harmon Wong Woo in Richmond, California. I told him I was in Redding, and would be in Richmond to see him the following day. He said, "Wayne, I am glad you called ahead. We are going on a trip in the morning. But we will delay our plans and wait for you here." We got there at about 3:30 in the afternoon and had dinner with his family. It was a joyous reunion after more than twenty years. He then guided us to Berkeley, where another uncle's and aunt's family lived. We stayed in San Francisco for three days, visiting friends and relatives. The next stop was Sacramento to visit more relatives and friends.

The next day we headed to Reno, Nevada. We stayed overnight because Kim had a friend as well as relatives there. We traveled the next day and spent the night at Evanston, Wyoming. The next day we arrived in Denver to visit friends and relatives for the night. The following day we returned to Wichita and arrived on September 2, just in time for Linda and David to begin the fall semester at Wichita State University. It was a memorable vacation trip that all of us enjoyed, and it will never be erased from our memories.

CHAPTER 6

❦ ❦ ❦   New Enterprises

Between 1968 and 1971 my family bought several commercial buildings. We bought a three-unit small strip center at East Harry and Rutan Street, which was our first commercial building. Then we bought our second three-unit commercial building at 322 West Harry Street. I discovered that managing commercial buildings, compared to apartments, was a lot easier. The tenants were more reliable, and there were fewer problems with the upkeep of the buildings because they were devoid of appliances or lawns.

By 1972 our children had grown up. Linda, after completing two years of college, was working in an insurance company. David was still in college but was also working at Boeing Aircraft Company, while Wilma had just graduated from Wichita State University with a teaching degree. She applied for jobs in the Wichita public school system but was never hired. Wilma believed it was racial discrimination that barred her from becoming a schoolteacher. She ended up working as a receptionist at a firm that manufactured uniforms, but she also held down two other part-time jobs at restaurants.[1] Edward was enrolled in West High School.

Kim was restless and bored at home. At forty-four years old, she had already raised a family. Life seemingly was now meaningless. One day she said to me, "Wayne, I want to go to work." Of course she had worked at the T-Bone, but that only lasted a few years. The job of a dishwasher lost its appeal for her. She craved another waged job. At that time we were living in our second home on South Water. Three blocks away was a commercial laundry company. Kim went down there and applied for a job and was immediately hired. I worked nights, so in the daytime I took her to work and picked her up at the end of the day. She completed her first working day there.

The next day, I said to her in the early morning, "Kim, are you ready to go to work?"

"No, I quit," she firmly replied. "I don't want to work in that place."

"What happened?" I asked, somewhat puzzled.

"Those machines, they keep coming, you have to stand there and fold. You have to fold because if you didn't fold fast enough it's going to pass you. I stood there and folded and folded. But there was no time to go the restroom and so I ended up urinating in my pants. I quit. I don't want to work in that company."

Kim Suey asked me to buy a restaurant so that she could have a job. Initially I considered the diner, Gracie's, on Harry Street, but the stubborn owner would not budge on the price. Then Dutch's on Washington Street became available, but it was just a little, dirty place. After searching for six months we bought the Georgie Porgie Pancake Shop from George Laham. The restaurant was located in Normandie Center on Central and Woodlawn. Normandie Center had a good mixture of stores, including the Safeway grocery store, TG&Y discount store, and Gessler Drug Store. The posh neighborhood of Eastborough was nearby and the surrounding area was still fairly new.

Laham was a shoe repairman who knew nothing about running a restaurant, and had to hire a woman to cook. She quit to go work at Beech. He demanded $50,000 for the property, but he was pulling in only $12,000 worth of business each month. I flatly told him that his property was only worth, at the most, twice that of his gross income. I offered $30,000 but he rejected it. I walked off, but three weeks later he called me and negotiated it upward to $35,000.

During the first few months business was slow, like the previous owners, and much to our consternation, we averaged about $12,000 a month in revenue. Between Kim and me, we cleared only $400 a month, which paled in comparison to the $600 a month I pulled in at the T-Bone. Therefore we changed the menu, kept the interior decoration, and then started doing better business.

The business kept us in a frantic rush. We served breakfast, lunch, and dinner. Breakfast was served all day, and buckwheat pancakes was the house specialty. We also served soups, sandwiches, steaks, meatloaf, seafood, and fried chicken. Each day we also served one special Chinese American dish, whether it be chow mein, shrimp fried rice, sweet and sour pork, or egg foo young. We opened six days a week and were closed on Mondays. The hours were long, from 7:00 A.M. to 9:00 P.M. However, I was used to the routine; not so Kim, who initially complained of tired muscles, a back problem, and dishpan hands. Eventually she got used to it, or at least complained less of it.

The restaurant was close to Eastborough, where the wealthy businesspeople, lawyers, doctors, and real estate developers lived. In the back of our dining room a big table seated ten people. That was a popular spot for meetings. These professional people typically came in at about 7:30 A.M., ordered breakfast, and visited with other professionals. After they ate their breakfasts, they left for work. The other professional stragglers continually came in to eat and chat until about 10:00 A.M.

Many significant real estate deals were sealed at the restaurant. Land developer George Ablah, who was a big-time mover, maker, and shaker, brought us a lot of business. One time a newspaper reported that Ablah had quipped, "I probably put together more deals at Georgie Porgie's and Sambo's [another local diner] than I have in my own office."[2] City commissioners and occasionally congressmen were known to have dropped by too.

Kim was in charge of the kitchen while I took care of the dining room and the rental properties. Kim and I worked well together—the years of collaborating at the T-Bone Supper Club came in handy; there was not a whole lot of bickering and fighting. We were respectful toward each other. In the kitchen, Kim devised a "system" to get around her inability to read English. When a waitress took an order, she would put it on a spindle and then the prep cooks would call out the orders so that Kim would know what to cook. Later I took the order tickets home and helped Kim learn to recognize the meanings of the words and phrases of the order items. Eventually we did the same thing with sale items in grocery store advertisements.[3]

Kim worked very hard in the kitchen. In the first year or so of the restaurant's operation, I relied on three cooks—two black and one white—who worked in shifts to prepare the American dishes. Kim, however, was a fast learner. Soon she knew how to prepare meatloaf, steaks, liver and onions, stews, pancakes, and assorted foods. She pounded the meat, deboned whole chickens, trimmed vegetables, cooked the food, and even washed dishes. At closing time each night she mopped the kitchen floor and cleaned kitchen counters. Today she has arthritis in her hands from those long days of heavy manual labor.

In the steamy kitchen, Edward gave a helping hand; when we started running Georgie Porgie he was already fifteen years old and could wash dishes, and eventually he learned to cook. By then he was the only child still living at home. In 1972 Linda and Wilma had moved to California, while David was attending Wichita State University. After completing college he was hired at Boeing as an electrical engineer, a position he still holds today.

Our philosophy in operating this restaurant was to provide high-quality food at reasonable prices, fast service, and a pleasant and friendly atmosphere. Because I had worked all those years in the kitchen, the dining room was a new "territory" to me. I had some difficulty adjusting to the new routine of greeting customers and attending to their needs. I was shy, and was even a little fearful of the prospect of having to talk to the customers. An old lady dripping in jewelry and dressed in finery—who became a regular—once told me, "Don't be nervous. They might have more money than you do, but they are just people. Just relax and be yourself." I appreciated her remarks very much. I soon got over my anxiety, and eventually remembered about 80 percent of customers' names. I greeted the customers by their first names. Today, some fourteen years after we sold our restaurant, I occasionally run into former customers at the grocery store and still call them by name.

The year after we took possession of Georgie Porgie, we bought our third house just two blocks from the rear of the restaurant. Instead of driving ten miles round-trip from our house to the restaurant, Kim now could simply walk to work. We sold our old house and invested our money in stocks.

In 1974, because we were far too busy at the restaurant to take care of our apartments, we sold the two duplexes and the nine-unit apartment. All of the proceeds were invested in income and growth stocks.

John Callahan was our legal counsel. He suggested forming a corporation to minimize our income tax liability. A corporation was taxed 25 percent of the income, whereas we were paying 36 percent at that time. Furthermore, he advised that we should live on our rental income and draw no salary from the corporation. Instead we should let the corporation accumulate its profits for future real estate investments. On July 9, 1975, Wong Enterprises Inc. was incorporated.

In 1978 I realized that in ten years I would be sixty-five years old. In order for me to draw a decent Social Security retirement check, I had to earn a substantial amount of money. So I started paying myself $2,500 a month, and Kim was paid $1,000 a month.

Lindy Andeel was a local real estate developer. In 1976 he told me that I should invest in real estate with triple net leases. Triple net meant that the tenant would pay all the taxes, insurance, and repairs. He said I should have the mortgages paid off in eight years. A percentage clause in the lease specified that over a certain amount of the gross sales, the tenant was required to pay an additional 6 percent as rent. He explained that he had a corner lot at the shopping center on 21st and Oliver Street for sale. He said that both Taco Tico and Sonic Drive-In would sign triple net leases for twenty years.[4] All I had to do was buy that corner lot and the bank would finance the loan to build those two stores. I thought that was an excellent investment. I bought that corner lot, borrowed the money from the bank, and built the two stores for Taco Tico and Sonic Drive-In. As it turned out, I paid off the bank loan in just five years.

On October 1, 1980, a real estate agent who dropped by regularly at Georgie Porgie for meals asked me if I would be interested in building a Quicktrip store with a triple net lease for twenty years. I jumped on the suggestion, and this became the first Quicktrip real estate built by Wong Enterprises Inc., with a 12 percent return on the investment.

On April 1, 1982, Jimmy Carter was president. Inflation in 1982 was rampant, with interest rates hovering between 18 and 22 percent. Quicktrip was anxious to expand, but money was hard to come by, and the corporation was only willing to pay 13 percent rent for the total cost of the land and building. The Quicktrip manager for the Wichita area asked me if I would be interested in building another store for them.

I did not believe that in the long run the interest rate would stay this high. I told him that if I could borrow the money I would do it. The total cost was $240,000.

I convinced Linda and David to join this venture, with each of us putting up $40,000. Larry Carney was at that time the president of Central Bank. He ate lunch at Georgie Porgie regularly. I asked him to loan me the other $120,000 to build the Quicktrip store at Central Street and Greenwich Road. He agreed. Linda, David, and I formed Mar Wong Enterprises, Inc. as an investment corporation and built the store for Quicktrip. In 1983 the owners of the Quicktrip store at 55th Street and South Broadway wanted to expand to twice its size, so we did the expansion for them.

President Carter lost his second-term election to Ronald Reagan in 1984. Under President Ronald Reagan, the economy expanded quickly. The interest rate steadily dropped to 7 percent. Our 13 percent return rate on our Quicktrip investment looked very attractive indeed. In the 1990s we continued to maintain our business ties to Quicktrip, helping it develop new gas stations as the city expanded in northeastern and western directions.

In April 1991 Kim, who had been in charge of the restaurant kitchen all these years, wanted to sell the Georgie Porgie and retire. We placed a "restaurant for sale" advertisement in the *Wichita Eagle* to attract attention. It worked. Joe Aoun, with eighteen years of experience running restaurants, decided to buy the establishment. We set September 1, 1991, as the closing day. Kim promised to stay for two weeks to help the new owner with kitchen operations, and I promised to hang around at the restaurant for three weeks to help him get acquainted with the customers.

Because our son Edward worked with us at the restaurant, we had to help him find a job to support his family of two children and a wife. We contacted some real estate brokers, informing them about our plan to look for some kind of fast food service to operate. Through these contacts I met Don Venhaus. Don had worked for Long John Silver as a regional supervisor for about twelve years. Tired of living out of a suitcase, Don wanted to work in town. After some lengthy discussions beginning in 1991, I, along with Edward and Don, ventured into running a Long John Silver franchise, with two restaurants. One was located in Wichita and another in Newton, Kansas. This franchise came in the wake of the earlier venture to build Taco Tico and Sonic Drive-In restaurants. Five years later in Wichita we opened our third Long John Silver restaurant. In 1994 we—Don, myself, and a number of other investors—opened a Spaghetti Jack's next to our Long John Silver, which happened to be only half a mile from the old T-Bone club. Every Sunday I dropped by Spaghetti Jack's to work for a few hours without pay; it was fun hanging out with the customers, some of whom had patronized our Georgie Porgie, while others remembered me from my earlier T-Bone days. Eventually we owned another Spaghetti Jack's restaurant on the city's west side.

As I grew older, I developed a passion for travel. In 1983 we closed our restaurant for a month to make the dream trip of our lifetimes—a China tour for twenty-one days. "The Trip of Our Dreams Come True," read the sign in front of our restaurant's display window, also announcing the month-long closure of the restaurant. By then China was no longer an isolated country closed to tourists. Foreign exchange was welcomed, as was economic development once the era of Mao Zedong ended with his death in 1976. I was eager to show my birthplace to my children.

We left Wichita on June 27 for Albany, California, where Linda lives. Wilma lives in El Cerrito, California, about a mile from her sister.

We—the entire family—left San Francisco on United Airlines on June 30, 1983, and arrived in Hong Kong on July 1. We flew from San Francisco to Hong Kong in twelve short hours, nonstop; when I went to China as a soldier nearly forty years ago, it took about sixty days of difficult travel by troop ship from Los Angeles to India.

The stay in Hong Kong lasted three nights, which gave us the chance to visit with my brother's and sister's families. It had been thirty-six years since we had bid farewell in May 1947. My brother has six children and my sister has one daughter. No doubt it was the most joyous, heartwarming, and exciting reunion all of us had experienced in some time. One of the simple tokens of remembrance received from us by everyone we encountered on the trip were these balloons lettered in

Chinese and English that proclaimed, "Long Live Chinese and American Friendship."

We left Hong Kong on July 4 by train to Guangzhou. My maternal uncle's family lived in Guangzhou. We planned to stay in that city for just one night, because the tour group would leave the following morning for Guilin. So all of our excited relatives came to the hotel to visit us. In Guilin we took in the stupendous landscape, which included the River Li and the Seven Star Caves.

On the morning of July 7 we flew to Hangzhou. We stayed there for two nights. The world-famous West Lake is in Hangzhou. Hangzhou is also renowned for its silk, embroidery, and pottery. We bought embroidered pictures and three hand-carved round coffee tables that were shipped to the United States.

We left that city by train to Shanghai on July 9 and enjoyed the sights of that metropolitan center for the next four days. We visited silk-weaving factories and cruised Shanghai Harbor. We shopped at the Friendship Store, where only tourist money was acccpted. There were two buses for our group—on one bus the tour guide spoke English for the benefit of the American-born children, and on the other bus the tour guide spoke Cantonese. We arrived in Beijing by air on July 12 and stayed there for three nights. We visited the Ming Tomb, marveled at the splendor of the Forbidden City, roamed the Emperor's summer palace, and walked the ancient Great Wall.

On July 15 we arrived back in Guangzhou at about noon. On this day we went to visit my uncle's place and my aunt's home. I invited them for a dinner banquet.

On July 16 I chartered a van in Guangzhou to take us back to my birthplace at Taishan. We do not have any immediate family members living there anymore. The housemaid that my mother raised had married and was taking care of our old house. She had six children, and one of the children was living in that house. It was an eye-opener for my children to see the level of "backwardness" of rural Chinese peasants' lives. These people were bereft of running water, electricity, and indoor toilets and lived in dilapidated houses.

On July 17 we left the village in a charter van to visit the birthplace

of Sun Yat Sen—the Father of the Chinese Republic—at Zhongshan.
From there we went to Macao, the Portuguese-owned territory. From
Macao we took the ferry to Hong Kong to visit again with my brother's
and sister's families. Kim also visited with her two other brothers who
at that time lived and worked in Hong Kong. Later Kim sponsored
these two brothers and their families to the United States.

From Hong Kong we returned to Wichita via San Francisco. It took
us two days of frantic preparation to get the restaurant opened again.
This was another trip we would never forget. When we opened our
restaurant again after being closed for four weeks we were very busy.
We were relieved and happy that we had not lost any business.[5]

After our retirement, which dated from the time we sold Georgie
Porgie, we have enjoyed even more the pursuit of traveling, me more
than Kim, however. Between 1990 and 2002 we took several overseas
vacations, such as a twelve-day trip to Hong Kong, Taishan, and Taiwan
in 1990, and a whirlwind tour of nine European countries in 1992. In
April 1992 we went on a leisurely ten-day Hawaiian cruise and had
an emotional reunion with my 987th Company commander, William
Ching, and his family.

In 2000 we headed off to Taishan for a special "Flying Tigers" reunion and cruised the Yangzi River. During the visit to Taishan, members of the Fourteenth Air Service Group and the Fourteenth Air Force
Association—organizations made up mostly of Chinese American
veterans—placed memorial floral wreaths before the Flying Tigers
monument located at Rock Flower Hills Park, Taishan. Built in 1991
with money raised wholly from Chinese American veterans, and then
expanded with a memorial gate, the granite and marble monument was
dedicated to the memory of all CBI veterans.[6] More recently, I headed
off in May 2002 to Beijing for a World War II veterans reunion.

Of all our trips since 1990, perhaps the most memorable and personal
one was the 1990 trip to Taishan. In 1988 the Oy Shee descendant who
was taking care of the family memorial building wrote to inform me
that the roof was in a terrible, leaky condition. It would cost about
$25,000 in Chinese Yuen (about U.S. $3,000) to remodel and repair
the roof. I believe the building was originally built in 1906. In 1935 my
granduncle Look Shew returned to the village from Penang, Malaya. He

remodeled and expanded the front half of the memorial. However, by then the back half of the building's roof was in dire need of repair.

As a result of World War II, those of us in America lost contact with descendants in Penang. I contacted all of the remaining overseas Bong Shui descendants to ask for contributions toward repair of that building. Thankfully, twenty-two descendants responded positively. In the end, I put up most of the money.

The repair, as well as remodeling, was completed in 1989. In the middle of April of that year, Chinese students demonstrated for reform and democracy at Tiananmen Square. The month-and-a-half standoff between students and government ended with the June 4, 1989, massacre of hundreds of students. Because of the unsettled sociopolitical situation, we decided to wait until 1990 to return to Changlong village for the memorial building's rededication.

On July 3, 1990, my real brother Henjung, my daughters Linda and Wilma, and I flew from San Francisco to Hong Kong. From Hong Kong we traveled with my sister Suit Wing, brother Ying Kam, and several other relatives by train to Guangzhou. From Guangzhou we left in a chartered van for the village. By prior arrangement my cousin Ying Park and his three daughters, who lived in Toronto, met us at the village for the dedication.

The next day our memorial service began with offerings to the family altar at the memorial building. After that stage, we went to the individual graves of deceased relatives to burn incense and paper money and to light firecrackers. We then came back to the memorial building for a seven-course feast for all the people of the village. An estimated 216 people attended the joyous celebrations. Overall, the trip gave me and my family the opportunity to show gratitude to our ancestors for the path they laid for us.

Final Reflections

My long years of life on this earth have been ones of contentment, love, and many joyful experiences. I also felt that my guardian angel had looked after and protected me many times over.

As stated at the outset of this autobiography, I fell a significant distance from a tree onto the ground when I was about seven or eight years old. Miraculously I regained consciousness. No bone was broken and I suffered from no other ill effects. In 1983 and again in 1990 when I and my family returned to visit my home village, I followed the Chinese tradition of making food offerings and burning incense and paper money to thank the Gods for protecting me and saving me from harm during that fall.

In earlier pages I detailed how I was, in the immediate postwar era, saved from drowning in a swimming pool in India. That was in itself a miracle. In 1946 I returned to China to visit my parents and family, and was scheduled to leave China in April 1947 with Kim. That March, in my native village, an incident happened to me that I shall never forget.

In China generally the village outdoor houses are grouped together about half a mile from the village. One morning I went to use our outdoor house, which was about nine feet wide and fifteen feet long. We also used this outdoor house to store rice straw and wood ashes as fertilizer. About one foot from the door, a hole about 6 ft. x 6 ft. x 3 ft. deep was dug to store the cow, pig, and human manure to be mixed with the ashes for fertilizer.

After I pulled my pants down, I squatted to defecate. Suddenly, I saw a large snake about three and a half inches in diameter crawl in from under the door. Then it raised its head, three feet above the ground. It was higher than I was in my squatted position. Its neck was flattened to the width of about four inches and its tongue was wagging in and out of its mouth. The snake, with its menacing eyes, squarely looked at me. I squatted there frozen, motionless, staring at it straight in the eye for about thirty seconds. Then the snake lowered itself to the ground and crawled toward the back of the outdoor house. I quickly pulled up my pants and ran out the door. I estimated the snake to be about twelve feet long, because its tail was about three feet from the front door.

I dashed home to get a shovel to kill the snake. I was about halfway home when I literally collided into our hired hand Done Gone. He asked me why I was running so fast. Breathless, I told him what had happened. He expressed the desire to capture that snake. So I picked up a shovel and he took an old blanket. Both of us headed back to the outdoor house. We opened the outdoor house. The reptile had already left. On the back side of these outdoor houses were a lot of trees and thick bushes. For about the next twenty minutes we both searched and beat the bushes to try to flush the snake out. There was no sign of the reptile. As the news about the appearance of the large snake spread, the people who lived near the outdoor house said they had lost some chickens in the last two days.

I took pride in myself for staying calm, making no provocative move to cause the snake to strike at me, and I was proud that I had out-stared the reptile. If I had tried to scare or fan off the snake, or made a threatening move toward that big animal, the outcome of this incident could have been quite different. I shudder to think what the outcome might have been. I had a strong feeling that my guardian angel had kept me safe again.

August 8 through 10, 1995, was the 54th CBI army reunion, which included members of the 987th Signal Company. The reunion was held in Seattle. The meeting was well organized and the weather beautiful. I was admitted into the United States through the Port of Seattle on January 3, 1936. That was almost sixty years ago. So many changes had happened in my life. I was elated to see how much Seattle had also changed.

At that reunion Lieutenant Colonel Thomas Lew and I shared a room at the Ramada Inn. One morning, I think it was August 9, we left the hotel together. Thomas pushed open the door, stepped past it, and stood on the curb. As I pushed past the door to walk onto the driveway, Thomas grabbed me and yelled, "Hey, Wayne, stop!" as a car at high speed passed by me and came to a screeching stop, missing me by inches. Had he not grabbed me from walking onto the driveway, I hate to think what would have become of me. By the grace of the Gods and the presence of Thomas Lew, I was saved from certain tragedy beyond calculation.

Today and every day as I continue to live on this earth, I am grateful for my productive life in the United States. The sacrifices of my ancestors have been many, and the present remains indebted to the past.

Appendix: Methodology

The genesis for this book project came in spring 2002. As a historian who then taught in the public history M.A. program at Wichita State University, Wichita, Kansas, I developed and taught several graduate-level courses offering students the opportunity to interact with nonacademic audiences while learning how to reclaim the history of both elites and the inarticulate. Such courses also covered critical themes in public history such as memory, public historical consciousness, vernacular culture, and self-constructed identities. That spring semester, for the first time, I introduced such themes into an upper-division undergraduate course, "Ethnic America in the Twentieth Century." That course also marked the start of my efforts to deepen my understanding of the function of autobiographies in validating identities, their place in Asian American historiography, and their ties to those pivotal themes in public history.

That class focused on the research and mounting of an exhibit at the Wichita Public Library entitled "Beyond Black and White: Hispanic and Asian Americans in Twentieth-Century Wichita" that eventually opened on May 11, 2002. As part of the preparation for the exhibit, I compiled a roster of individuals who might be suitable subjects for oral history interviews. One of the persons suggested by Barbara Hammond of the local Sedgwick County Historical Society was Wayne Hung Wong, who had immigrated to Wichita from China in the 1930s. Hammond graciously verbally shared with me the outline of her informal interview with Wong. However, she warned me—and this was the first sign that the autobiography had inherent inconsistencies—that Wong's recollections were self-selective; it took considerable efforts on her part to elicit any information from him pertaining to racial discrimination.

I then spoke with Wong and read his legible, approximately fifty-page handwritten memoir, parts of which Hammond had lightly edited and also typed. Even though the handwritten text exhibited grammatical, syntax, and spelling errors, the content was nevertheless riveting reading. I knew then that this was an important work documenting important elements of Chinese immigrant life in the Midwest since the 1930s. The two-hour interview of Wong I conducted for the purpose of the exhibit initiated a process Michael Frisch identifies as the linking of authorship and interpretive authority. This "shared authority," as he calls it, played out as I, through a series of open-ended questions, led Wong into his past, and he began to reveal suppressed aspects of that past, and I in turn examined these recollections with my "interpretive lens."[1]

In the spring of 2003 I taught a graduate-level class in documentary editing. I assigned the ten enrolled students the task of interviewing Wong and his children. Regrettably, Wong's spouse, Yee Kim Suey, refused to be interviewed; I suspect that like many other ordinary Americans she did not consider her experiences as significant or worth sharing with the reading public. These new interviews of Wong, his daughter Wilma, and son David were further evidence that much was left unsaid in the original autobiography.

The initial interview, as well as the follow-up interviews in the spring of 2003—which lasted a total of twelve hours—revealed to me that there was a disjuncture between Wong's initial recollections of his past and the historical truth. Wong's past, as documented in his writing, was clearly a cultural, constructed artifact, a selective memory no less.

Given what scholars of memory have uncovered, it is not surprising that Wong in his early version of the autobiography did not mention at all the instances of racial discrimination he and his family experienced in Wichita, Kansas. (See the introductory essay for a discussion of such instances of prejudice.) As such, he could insist that he had experienced hardly any racial discrimination in Wichita, although later interviews revealed he and his family did experience hostility both within and without Wichita. Donald A. Ritchie's comment that it is common for interviewees to suppress painful or unpleasant memories and to revert to nostalgia seems to apply to the Wong case.[2]

I was well aware of Frisch's reminder that contemporary contexts and pressures "operate as a sort of rearguard attack on the structure of memory."[3] The construction of a memory takes place not in isolation, but in contexts of community, broader politics, and social dynamics.[4] Any recollection is prompted by a present need or circumstance, and that recollection can change as a new need or circumstance arises.[5]

Wong's memory of the past developed in the context of specific circumstances, of the historical legacy of Orientalism, the contemporary understanding of Asian Americans as the model minority, and the pressures of social incorporation. The dominant plot in Wong's memory was the story of progress, of change for the better. Wong relied on his understanding of the past to lay claim to his identity as an American, a "paper son" who turned out to be a good citizen. David Lowenthal writes that those who tamper with history sometimes do so to show their faith in progress.[6] I contend that Lowenthal's rejoinder here applies to Wong's circumstances.

I shared the students' interviews with Wong, drawing his attention to either the absence or inadequate coverage of certain themes in his autobiography that surfaced during those interviews, such as the background of his parents, the operational details of the Pan-American Café, his reaction to the Pearl Harbor attack, service in the U.S. Army, marriage to Kim Suey, family life in the 1940s through the 1960s, the transnational ties to China in the postwar era, labor in the family-owned restaurant, the second-generational dilemma faced by his children, and as well, of course, the lack of articulation of racial conflict.

The "silences" that exist in Wong's early version of his memoirs remind me of what historian Sucheng Chan uncovered during the course of editing Mary Paik Lee's *Quiet Odyssey: A Pioneer Korean Woman in America* (1990). Chan argues that Lee wrote her autobiography as an act of reconciling the tensions of being both a Christian (and I might add, being an American) and an Asian immigrant in the United States. That motivation, as implied in Chan's analysis of the work, led to the adoption of a paradoxical position on racial discrimination. Though Lee recounted numerous instances of racial prejudices inflicted upon her or her family, she also made a number of "ingratiating statements," or expressed her gratitude for the small gestures of kindness extended to her. As an Asian immigrant, she undoubtedly suffered much ill treatment at the hands of non-Asians. Yet Lee never lost her faith in "what the United States *could* be." By holding onto such a vision or faith Lee and other similar early Asian immigrants were able to lead their lives in a racialized world with some modicum of integrity and strength.[7] Similarly, Wong wrote his memoirs, I suspect, as a way to reconcile his fraudulent, perhaps even troubled, past with a respected present.

At my urging, Wong then rewrote his autobiography, incorporating most of the once-suppressed or undeveloped themes. The end result was a much longer text that is wider in its coverage of personal, family, and community histories. Instead of a story with a straightforward trajectory of an individual who immigrated to the United States and made a good life for himself, various layers of his historical experiences are woven in, creating a more complex narrative.

To support Wong's narrative, place it in its proper historical context, and counter some misleading facts or inaccurate details in it, I gleaned relevant information from archival materials. Paul Williams, a graduate student, and I conducted research at the San Bruno (California) branch of the National

Archives and Record Services. We located immigration records for Wong; his paper father and several paper brothers; his biological father; and Yee, his wife. To locate the appropriate files, four major collections were consulted: Arrival Investigation Case Files, 1884–1944; Certificates of Identity for Chinese Residents, 1909–c. 1946; Passenger Lists of Vessels Arriving in San Francisco, California, 1893–1953; and Lists of Chinese Passengers Arriving in San Francisco, California, 1881–1914.

In Wichita several graduate students assisted in conducting appropriate research in local archives. Newspaper articles provided insights into the small Chinese community in Wichita before World War II, as well as the nature of the public school system that Wong attended. Several articles also highlighted (as well as "exotified") the history of the Chinese American restaurants in the city. The lack of any indexes for any of the major newspapers made such research difficult, but we were able to utilize the public library's "clipping cards," which were microfilmed copies of compiled articles arranged by subject matter. The library's Sanborn fire insurance maps showed the dimensions of the Pan-American Café and other downtown restaurants. County real estate records showed that Wong's father never owned the restaurant building and was most likely a tenant. A search for school records was unrewarding; though an archive exists for such records, yearbooks for Wong's schooling days were apparently never retained. However, Wong's copy of his elementary school report card and letters of commendation from teachers in the middle high and high schools provided sufficient proof of his attendance at these institutions.

The microfilm edition of the U.S. census schedules for 1920 and 1930, as well as schedules for a state census for 1925, though flawed owing to undercounting and possible racial biases shaping the enumerators' work, offered some documentation of the whereabouts of a few of Wong's clanspeople as well as their domiciles. For example, the U.S. census schedules for 1920 showed that eight Chinese lived at 150 North Market, the address for the Pan-American Café. All of them bore the family name "Mar," which is also Wong's real family name. However, I was not able to ascertain with veracity using the 1920 census that the Pan-American Café had been established by 1920 because the name of the restaurant did not appear in the schedules; neither were the workers' occupations identified in the schedules. The 1930 schedules revealed that at least five Mars lived in that city, all near the 150 North Market address, though oddly, none at that precise one.

My students and I studied city directories published for the years 1917 to 1945. These provided addresses of the restaurants, names of workers listed under the names of those premises, and sometimes the occupations of those men. The directories also provided proof that the Pan-American Café had been in operation at least since 1920, and possibly even a little earlier. By studying both the directories and contemporaneous city maps, I figured out the spatial distribution of the restaurants and matched that to earlier findings of the fire insurance maps. The directories also allowed me to verify Wong's places of employment in the postwar years, though the incompleteness of such documents meant that at times gaps exist in the corroborating evidence.

The above and other culled information appears in this book as footnotes for the autobiography's text. Rather than replace the inaccuracies in the text with the correct information, which would have tampered with Wong's writing, the corrections are in the footnotes. In so doing, I also draw the reader's attention to one limitation of oral histories and autobiographies: human memory is fallible, and as such, recollections are sometimes inaccurate or incomplete.

Next I turned my attention to editing the text of the autobiography itself. Wong writes lucidly, with events outlined in a fairly chronological order. My goal in editing this work was to increase its readability. Because Wong wrote the autobiography during a number of sessions over the course of several years, some repetition of ideas and themes crept into it; my first task was to strike out such duplicated material. To facilitate a good flow of the prose, I combined short, choppy sentences into longer ones. I broke up long paragraphs that featured several ideas or themes into shorter ones, and then moved sentences around to increase the thematic coherence of the paragraphs. Sometimes I reordered the sequence of events to give the narrative an even tighter chronological organization. The original manuscript was a run-on text, so I divided it into chapters and provided titles for them, although one of them, significantly, was provided by Wong himself in his handwritten manuscript, namely "In the Army" (chapter 3). Whenever necessary I made grammatical and spelling corrections; however, Wong had been most methodical in putting down his thoughts on paper, so much so that such errors did not appear in every sentence. Finally, I replaced words and phrases that were used far too often with synonyms or an alternative way of expressing those ideas.

Influenced by Chan, I edited the text substantively, besides making stylistic changes. I agree with Chan that it is important that the attitude of the autobiographer toward the various people he or she comes in contact with "be captured as accurately as possible."[8] With that in mind, I chose not to delete the vigorous assertion that he had been treated with much kindness throughout his life in Wichita, and that compared to the other places he had visited, Wichita had inflicted very little racial prejudice on him and his family. For the same reason of capturing his subjective consciousness, I chose not to delete the last chapter entitled "Reflections," in which Wong offers his gratitude for having enjoyed a productive and secure life even though it might come across to some readers as paradoxically out of place, because Wong's early life was not devoid of adversity. To some extent, it is precisely that kind of adversity that has fostered Wong's overall positive disposition about life in America, one that has enabled him to survive in a white-dominated world.

I did remove certain short paragraphs or sentences from the original manuscript. These mostly had to do with names of people that Wong referred to in passing but who never were mentioned again in the text. Influenced by Chan's editing process, I also chose to delete several events Wong related that he had heard secondhand. The only ones that I retained dealt with the discrimination encountered by his Chinese American peers in the army; though I could not find corroborating evidence for those several incidents, the vividness of the stories suggest a certain level of veracity. I also retained them because there are still only a few accounts of such ill treatment of Chinese American soldiers in wartime United States.

Admittedly, from the beginning of this process I was far less interested in Wong's business dealings in the late twentieth century; perhaps my "bias" was shaped by my lack of interest in any part of the autobiography that did not converge with Asian American history. That said, my decision to condense this section, which appears in chapter 6, was also prompted by another obvious reason: to excise information of little interest to readers.

In regard to the transliteration of Chinese names, words, and phrases, I changed all proper nouns that were originally in the Cantonese dialect to conform to the pinyin romanization system that scholars, and increasingly the general public, are familiar with. However, for words and phrases commonly expressed in the Cantonese dialect, I used the Cantonese spelling. Names of people that appear in historical sources in the Cantonese spelling remain as such in this work, as do names of Wong's family members, kinfolk, and Chinese acquaintances.

I chose the title for this book. The original handwritten manuscript was entitled "Why Did I Live in Wichita for 65 Years?" I told Wong that a change of title was necessary because his autobiography covered more than just his life in Wichita, to which he heartily agreed. I initially chose *From Changlong to Wichita: The Memoir of a Chinese Immigrant.* One of the readers of this manuscript suggested a change of title that better reflected the themes of this book. I finally settled on *American Paper Son: A Chinese Immigrant in the Midwest* to point out three important themes in the life of Wong and his family: the legacy of exclusion that gave rise to the paper son phenomenon, the struggle to find acceptance as an American citizen, and the subjective consciousness that shaped the writing of this work.

Notes

Introduction

1. The term "paper son" refers to Chinese men who resorted to a fraudulent scheme that admitted them into the United States in spite of the exclusionary laws barring Chinese immigration. A more detailed explanation follows in this chapter.

2. Quote in Erika Lee, *At America's Gates: Chinese Immigration during the Exclusion Era, 1882–1943* (Chapel Hill: University of North Carolina Press, 2003), 22.

3. Published Chinese American autobiographies include Jade Snow Wong, *Fifth Chinese Daughter* (New York: Harper & Row, 1950); Pardee Lowe, *Father and Glorious Descendant* (Boston: Little, Brown, 1943); Tung Pok Chin with Winifred C. Chin, *Paper Son: One Man's Story* (Philadelphia: Temple University Press, 2000); Louise Leung Larson, *Sweet Bamboo: A Memoir of a Chinese American Family* (Berkeley: University of California Press, 1989); Lisa See, *On Gold Mountain: The One-Hundred-Year Odyssey of a Chinese-American Family* (New York: St. Martin's Press, 1995).

4. Archana J. Bhatt, "Asian Indians and the Model Minority Narrative: A Neocolonial System," in *The Emerging Monoculture: Assimilation and the "Model Minority,"* ed. Eric Mark Kramer (Westport, Conn.: Praeger, 2003), first quote in 207, 212–13; second quote in Ronald Takaki, *Strangers from a Different Shore: A History of Asian Americans,* 2d ed. (Boston: Little, Brown, 1998), 478.

5. Sharon M. Lee and Barry Edmonston, "The Socioeconomic Status and Integration of Asian Immigrants," in *Immigration and Ethnicity: The Integration of America's Newest Arrivals,* ed. Barry Edmonston and Jeffrey S. Passel (Washington, D.C.: Urban Institute Press, 1994), 124–25; see also Timothy P. Fong, *Asian American Experience: Beyond the Model Minority* (Upper Saddle River, N.J.: Prentice Hall, 1998), 56–68.

6. See James R. Shortridge, *The Middle West: Its Meaning in American Culture* (Lawrence: University Press of Kansas, 1989).

7. Wayne Patterson, "Introduction," in Easurk Emsen Charr, *The Golden Mountain: The Autobiography of a Korean Immigrant, 1895–1960,* ed. with an introduction by Wayne Patterson (Urbana: University of Illinois Press, 1996), xxx. See the Appendix for a parallel example in Mary Paik Lee's *Quiet Odyssey: A Pioneer Korean Woman in America,* ed. with an introduction by Sucheng Chan (Seattle: University of Washington Press, 1990). I am grateful to Roger Daniels for drawing my attention to this pivotal argument in Patterson's essay.

8. The classic work that interpreted the immigrant experience as one of uprootedness and alienation is Oscar Handlin's *The Uprooted* (Boston: Little, Brown, 1941).

9. See Yong Chen, *Chinese San Francisco, 1850–1943: A Trans-Pacific Community* (Stanford, Calif.: Stanford University Press, 2000); Madeline Hsu, *Dreaming of Gold, Dreaming of Home: Transnationalism and Migration Between the United States and South China, 1882–1943* (Stanford, Calif.: Stanford University Press, 2000); Lee, *At America's Gates.*

10. For the impact of both the Chinese Exclusion Act of 1882 and judiciary decisions on Chinese female immigration, see Sucheng Chan, "The Exclusion of Chinese Women, 1870–1943," in *Entry Denied: Exclusion and the Chinese Community in America, 1882–1943,* ed. Sucheng Chan (Philadelphia: Temple University Press, 1991), 94–146.

11. See Xiaojian Zhao, *Remaking Chinese America: Immigration, Family, and Community, 1940–1965* (New Brunswick, N.J.: Rutgers University Press, 2002), 33.

12. Studies that portray immigrants as worldly and forward-looking, and who had received some exposure to capitalism, include Yong Chen, "Internal Origins to Chinese Immigration Reconsidered," *Western Historical Quarterly* 25 (Winter 1997): 538–41; Haiming Liu, "The Social Origins of Early Chinese Immigrants: A Revisionist Perspective," in *The Chinese in America: A History from Gold Mountain to the New Millennium,* ed. Susie Lan Cassel (Walnut Creek, Calif.: Altamira Press, 2002), 2–16. For transnational ties, see Hsu, *Dreaming of Gold, Dreaming of Home;* Adam McKeown, *Chinese Migrant Networks and Cultural Change: Peru, Chicago, Hawaii, 1900–1945* (Chicago: University of Chicago Press, 2001).

13. Him Mark Lai, "The Guangdong Historical Background, with Emphasis on the Development of the Pearl River Delta Region," in *Chinese America: History and Perspectives 1991* (San Francisco: Chinese Historical Society of America, 1991), 88.

14. This estimate is from Mae M. Ngai, "Legacies of Exclusion: Illegal Chinese

Immigration during the Cold War Years," *Journal of American Ethnic History* 18 (Fall 1978): 28.

15. See Zhao, *Remaking Chinese America,* 33. The "paper son" scheme is also analyzed in Lee, *At America's Gates,* 194–95, 203–7; Mae Ngai, *Impossible Subjects: Illegal Aliens and the Making of Modern America* (Princeton, N.J.: Princeton University Press, 2004), 204–6.

16. Lee, *At America's Gates,* 74, 84; quote in Ngai, *Impossible Subjects,* 205.

17. See case no. 22969/6-19, Arrival Investigation Case Files, 1844–1944, National Archives—Pacific Sierra Region, San Bruno, Calif.

18. For a discussion of the immigration-clearance process, and the reaction of Chinese detainees to the unfair treatment, see Lee, *At America's Gates,* 111–50. For the history of the Angel Island Immigration Station, see Him Mark Lai, Genny Lim, and Judy Yung, *Island: Poetry and History of Chinese Immigrants on Angel Island, 1910–1940* (San Francisco: Hoc Doi, 1986).

19. See Zhao, *Remaking Chinese America,* 86.

20. Philip Q. Yang, "Sojourners or Settlers: Post-1965 Chinese Immigrants," *Journal of Asian American Studies* 2, no. 1 (1999): 64.

21. Ngai, "Legacies of Exclusion," 3–35.

22. The term "coethnic" means members of the same ethnic community, which in the context of this book were the Chinese.

23. David I. MacLeod, *The Age of the Child: Children in America, 1890–1920* (New York: Twayne Publishers, 1998), 101; Benson Tong, "The Worldview of Asian American Children," in *Asian American Children: A Historical Guide,* ed. Benson Tong (Westport, Conn.: Greenwood Press), forthcoming.

24. For Hop Alley, see Huping Ling, "'Hop Alley': Myth and Reality of the St. Louis Chinatown, 1860s–1930s," *Journal of Urban History* 28 (January 2002): 184–219.

25. Bureau of the Census, *1980 Census of Population, vol. 1, Characteristics of the Population, Part 18, Kansas* (Washington, D.C., 1982), 22.

26. Erika Lee makes a similar argument for the situation in Buffalo, New York, in the early twentieth century. See Erika Lee, "'Wily John Chinaman' and 'Real American Chinese': Conflicting Images of Chinese Immigrants in Early-Twentieth-Century Buffalo, New York," in Conference on the 50th Anniversary of the Repeal of the Exclusion Acts, *The Repeal and Its Legacy: Proceedings of the Conference on the 50th Anniversary of the Repeal of the Exclusion Acts, November 12–14, 1993,* ed. Chinese Historical Society of America and Asian American Studies, San Francisco State University (San Francisco: Chinese Historical Society of America and Asian American Studies, San Francisco State University, 1994), 81–85.

27. Maurine Hung, "Chinese Without a Chinatown" (Ph.D. diss., University of Wisconsin–Milwaukee, 1988), 81–82; Roger Daniels, *Asian America: Chinese and Japanese in the United States since 1850* (Seattle: University of Washington Press, 1988), 68, 70.

28. Stephen H. Sumida, "East of California: Points of Origin in Asian American Studies," *Journal of Asian American Studies* 1, no. 1 (1998): 85.

29. Bureau of the Census, *Abstract of the Fourteenth Census of the United States, 1920* (Washington, D.C., 1923), 98; Bureau of the Census, *Fifteenth Census of the United States, 1930, Population, Volume II; General Report & Statistics by Subjects* (Washington, D.C., 1933), 41.

30. Bureau of the Census, *Twelfth Census of the United States, Taken in the Year 1900, Population Part II, Volume II* (Washington, D.C., 1902), xx; Bureau of the Census, *Fifteenth Census of the United States, 1930, Population, Volume II; General Report & Statistics by Subject* (Washington, D.C. 1933), 41; Bureau of the Census, *Sixteenth Census of the United States, Population, 1940, Volume II; United States Summary and Alabama–District of Columbia* (Washington, D.C., 1943), 52.

31. Sumida, "East of California," 94; Lisa Lowe, *Immigrant Acts: On Asian American Cultural Politics* (Durham, N.C.: Duke University Press, 1996), 4; the racialized black-white binary and how Asians contest those categories of difference is explained in Gary Y. Okihiro, *Common Ground: Reimagining American History* (Princeton, N.J.: Princeton University Press, 2001), 28–54; see also Gary Y. Okihiro, *Margins and Mainstreams: Asians in American History and Culture* (Seattle: University of Washington Press, 1994), 31–63.

32. Okihiro, *Common Ground,* 51.

33. Victor Jew, "'Chinese Demons': The Violent Articulation of Chinese Otherness and Interracial Sexuality in the U.S. Midwest, 1885–1889," *Journal of Social History* 37, no. 2 (2003): 389–410.

34. See Julie Courtwright, "A Slave to Yellow Peril: The 1886 Chinese Ouster Attempt in Wichita, Kansas," *Great Plains Quarterly* 22 (Winter 2002): 23–33; see also Craig Miner, *Wichita, the Magic City: An Illustrated History* (Wichita, Kans.: Wichita–Sedgwick County Historical Museum Association, 1988), 98–99.

35. Eleanor Wong Telamaque's semiautobiographical novel, *It's Crazy to Stay Chinese in Minnesota* (Nashville, Tenn.: Thomas Nelson, 1978), tells the story of a young girl who in the early twentieth century grew up in a small midwestern town. Though she did not experience any overt racial discrimination, she felt keenly the notion of being a racial novelty in that town. In the mid-twentieth century, the most virulent expression of anti-Asian prejudice

in the Midwest occurred when Japanese Americans were relocated from the internment camps to the Midwest, either for education or work. See Andrew B. Wertheimer, "Admitting Nebraska's Nisei: Japanese American Students at the University of Nebraska, 1942–1945," *Nebraska History* 83 (Summer 2002): 58–72; Leslie A. Ito, "Japanese American Women and the Student Relocation Movement, 1942–1945," *Frontiers: A Journal of Women Studies* 21, no. 3 (2000): 1–17.

36. K. Scott Wong, "The Meaning of Military Service to Chinese Americans during WWII," in *Duty & Honor: A Tribute to Chinese American World War II Veterans of Southern California,* ed. Marjorie Lee (Los Angeles: Chinese Historical Society of Southern California, 1998), 7–13; Peter Phan, "Familiar Strangers: The Fourteenth Air Service Group Case Study of Chinese American Identity During World War II," in *Chinese America: History and Perspectives, 1993* (San Francisco: Chinese Historical Society of America, 1993), 85–86.

37. William F. Strobridge, "In the Beginning . . .", in Lee, ed., *Duty & Honor,* 3.

38. Wong, "Meaning of Military Service to Chinese Americans," 8.

39. Ibid.; Christina M. Lim and Sheldon H. Lim, "In the Shadow of the Tiger: The 407th Air Service Squadron, Fourteenth Air Force, CBI, World War II," in *Chinese America: History and Perspectives 1993* (San Francisco: Chinese Historical Society of America, 1993), 30.

40. See Frank H. Wu, *Yellow: Race in America Beyond Black and White* (New York: Basic Books, 2002), 10–12. Gary Okihiro argues that race relations in the United States is defined as bipolar—between black and white—and Asians are "somewhere along the divide between black and white." See Okihiro, *Margins and Mainstreams,* 33–34.

41. Other instances of racial discrimination inflicted on Chinese American servicemen during the war years are recounted in Christina M. Lim and Sheldon M. Lim, *In the Shadow of the Tiger, the 407th Air Service Squadron, Fourteenth Air Service Group, Fourteenth Air Force, World War II* (Sacramento, Calif.: Griffin Printing, 1993), 7, 20.

42. Ibid., 52.

43. Phan, "Familiar Strangers," 89–91; see also Lim and Lim, *In the Shadow of the Tiger,* 51–53.

44. Ibid., 93.

45. Ibid., 93–94.

46. To date, Zhao's *Remaking Chinese America* is the only scholarly work on Chinese American families in the immediate postwar era.

47. Zhao, *Remaking Chinese America,* 133, 137; Judy Yung, *Chinese Women of*

America: A Pictorial History (Seattle: University of Washington Press, 1986), 81.

48. For second-generation Chinese Americans in the postwar era, see Gloria Heyung Chun, *Of Orphans and Warriors: Inventing Chinese American Culture and Identity* (New Brunswick, N.J.: Rutgers University Press, 2000), 71–96.

49. The concept of "cultural tourism" and its shaping force on identities are explored in Andrea Louie, "When You are Related to the 'Other': Relocating the Chinese Homeland in Asian American Politics through Cultural Tourism," *Journal of Asian American Studies* 11, no. 3 (2003): 735–63.

Chapter 1: Coming to America

1. In the nineteenth century, Taishan County, which lies on the southern coast of Guangdong, featured tree-covered hills that served as an obstacle to commercial agriculture and to the building of infrastructure for economic development. Devoid of natural waterways and rich alluvial soil, Taishan was unable to duplicate the economic success of the counties east of it in the fertile Pearl River delta. See Madeline Yuan-yin Hsu, *Dreaming of Gold, Dreaming of Home: Transnationalism and Migration Between the United States and South China, 1882–1943* (Stanford, Calif.: Stanford University Press, 2000), 19.

2. Wong's genealogical account is delineated in more detail in Mah Moon Gain, "Summary of the History of the Mah Family," unpublished essay, Mah Society of Calgary, Canada, copy in Wayne Wong personal papers. The reference to migration from the north parallels historical accounts of a larger movement of people—known as the Yue people—from the north to the south some three thousand years ago in Chinese history, giving rise to a distinctive regional culture—Cantonese—in Guangdong with surnames that are far less prevalent elsewhere. Wayne Hung Wong's family, being Cantonese, trace their history to these roots. See Him Mark Lai, "The Guangdong Historical Background, with Emphasis on the Development of the Pearl River Delta Region," in *Chinese America: History and Perspectives 1991* (San Francisco: Chinese Historical Society of America, 1991), 88.

3. A study conducted in the 1890s revealed that two-thirds of the Taishanese earned at least a part of their livelihoods from farming. Other typical means of living included fishing and production of cotton cloth, salt, sugar, tea, and noodles. See Hsu, *Dreaming of Gold, Dreaming of Home*, 21.

4. The immigration of the Chinese to Malaya was part of a larger worldwide diaspora of 2.5 million Chinese during the period from circa 1840 to 1900 to Southeast Asia, Africa, Australia, New Zealand, Hawaii, the West Indies, and

the Americas. See Sing-Wu Wang, *The Organization of Chinese Emigration, 1848–1888* (San Francisco: Chinese Materials Center, 1978), 8–9. In the British colony of Malaya, most Chinese were laborers, while a minority rose to become tradespeople, entrepreneurs, and compradores. See Victor Purcell, *The Chinese in Malaya* (London: Oxford University Press, 1967).

5. Footbinding was practiced in China from about the twelfth century to the beginning of the twentieth century. Young girls were subjected to tight bandages around their feet so as to facilitate the breaking of the arches, the bending of the toes, and the whole foot reduced in length to just a few inches. Bound feet were considered a sign of beauty, gentility, and eroticism, and as such increased the "value" of the girls in the marriage market. See Howard S. Levy, *Chinese Footbinding: The History of a Curious Erotic Custom* (New York: Walton Rawls, 1966). The practice, however, was far less common among peasant women because it restricted their mobility, and thus hindered labor in the fields. Undoubtedly, Wong's great-grandmother was in a privileged class. Typically, only the scholar-gentry, merchant, and landowner classes could afford the practice.

6. Christian missionaries initiated formal education for young Chinese women through the establishment of girls' schools, mostly in eastern coastal cities that were susceptible to Westernization in the wake of the Opium Wars (1839–1842; 1856–1860). From the late nineteenth century onward, Chinese reformers, both men and women, expanded these early efforts as well as agitated for an end to footbinding. See Ono Kazuko, *Chinese Women in a Century of Revolution, 1850–1950* (Stanford, Calif.: Stanford University Press, 1989), 28–29; also see Fan Hong, *Footbinding, Feminism and Freedom: The Liberation of Women's Bodies in Modern China* (London: Frank Cass, 1997), 50–69.

7. Mar Bong Shui's business dealings suggest the operations of a *jinshangzhuang,* or "Gold Mountain firms," that had close ties to Chinese businesses abroad. *Jinshangzhuang* took orders for Chinese goods and arranged for their shipment to overseas Chinese communities. They also facilitated the movement of correspondence and money between those communities and kinfolk in China. See Hsu, *Dreaming of Gold, Dreaming of Home,* 34–35.

8. In the traditional Chinese patrilineal and patrilocal household, the sons were also deemed more important than the daughters because the former could help with farm work. Daughters, however, were married off in late adolescence at a considerable expense. See Lloyd E. Eastman, *Family, Fields, and Ancestors: Constancy and Change in China's Social and Economic History, 1550–1949* (New York: Oxford University Press, 1988), 20.

9. *Jinshan* in Mandarin.

10. Ever since *United States v Mrs. Gun Lim* (1900), Chinese merchants could bring their wives into the country as part of the exempt classes. That judicial decision was then upheld in *Chang Chan et al. v John Nagle* (1925). *Tsoi Sim v United States* (1902) established the right of an alien wife of an American citizen to reside with her husband, and therefore that entitled her to land. This right was negated by the implications of the Immigration Act of 1924 until the passage of a new law in 1930 that partially restored that right. See Xiaojian Zhao, *Remaking Chinese America: Immigration, Family, and Community, 1940–1965* (New Brunswick, N.J.: Rutgers University Press, 2002), 13, 16–17.

11. The sex ratio was at its widest disparity in 1890: the male-to-female ratio was 27:1. Between 1900 and 1940, the era when most of Wong's immediate male relatives left for the United States, the sex ratio in Chinese America did improve toward gender parity. However as late as 1940, the male-to-female ratio was still 3:1. Statistics based on data from Judy Yung, *Unbound Feet: A Social History of Chinese Women in San Francisco* (Berkeley: University of California Press, 1995), 293.

12. Mar Tung Jing, whose paper name was Jee See Wing, arrived at the port of San Francisco on July 7, 1922. His return preceded the birth of his real son, Wayne Hung Wong, because the latter's actual birthdate was December 30, 1922. See case file no. 21266/4-4, Arrival Investigation Case Files, 1884–1944, National Archives—Pacific Sierra Region, San Bruno, Calif.

13. The chaos here refers to the sociopolitical turmoil engendered by warlordism. Following the downfall of the Qing dynasty in 1911, a crisis in early republican political authority led to the rise of warlordism by the early 1920s, an era that stretched into the 1930s when individual military commanders in various regions of China exercised autonomous political power and the central government was ineffectual. In Guangdong, the Yunnan army, led by a series of generals, encroached upon the power of various smaller armies led by local military leaders; this jostling for power laid ruin to farms and villages and led to exactions and onerous taxation. See Hsi-hseng Chi, *The Chinese Warlord System: 1916 to 1928* (Washington, D.C.: Center for Research in Social Systems, 1969), 73–74.

14. Ever since the passage of the Chinese Exclusion Act of 1882, only the exempt classes (merchants, diplomats, teachers, students, and travelers) could enter the United States. The entry of Chinese laborers was barred. The occupation of "bill collector" met the definition of a merchant. However, See Wing did not enter as a bill collector; his paper father did (see following note).

15. Jee See Wing entered the United States accompanied by his paper father, Jee Young Chung, one of sixteen owners and the bookkeeper (this occupa-

tion is probably what Wong meant by "bill collector") of the Quong Fook Chung mercantile store in Oakland, California. See Wing entered as the son of a merchant—a status deemed part of the exempt classes as ruled in *United States v Mrs. Gun Lim* (1900). Both of them were admitted into the United States on August 16, 1922—forty days after their ship, *Tjileboet,* docked in San Francisco. This delay was quite routine; some new arrivals spent months on the Angel Island Immigration Station before they were admitted or, in a few cases, deported. For a narrative of a case that was similar to See Wing's claimed status of son of a merchant but that resulted in a delay of two months because of noncorroborating testimonies, see Julia Fong, "The Fong Family History: Stories of My Father's Side of the Family," *Chinese America: History and Perspectives 1999* (San Francisco: Chinese Historical Society of America, 1999), 49–51. In 1924, in a case related to another paper son of Young Chung's that ended in deportation, the latter claimed that See Wing had left for Pittsburgh, Pennsylvania, some time in July or August 1923 to seek better economic opportunities. See case no. 22969/6-19, Arrival Investigation Case Files, 1844–1944, National Archives—Pacific Sierra Region, San Bruno, Calif.

16. In California, the immigrants who hailed from Taishan were heavily involved in laundries, small retail shops, and restaurants. See Thomas W. Chinn, Him Mark Lai, and Philip P. Choy, *A History of the Chinese in California: A Syllabus* (San Francisco: Chinese Historical Society of America, 1969), 4.

17. The first time a name that resembled Jee See Wing's appeared in the city directories was in 1926. A "Mar, Gee" was listed as a cook at the Pan-American Café. According to Wayne Wong, his father for a long time was under the wrong impression that his paper surname was "Gee." For some reason, he used his paper surname in combination with his real surname. "Gee Mar" was also listed living at 150 North Market in the 1925 Kansas census along with his cousin King Mar and six other people with "Mar" as surname. Neither did "Jee [or Gee], See Wing" nor "Mar Tung Jing" appear in the directories from 1922 to 1941. A "Gee, Sui Wing" did appear in the 1939 and 1941 issues, and was identified as a cook at that restaurant; most likely this was Wayne's father. See *R. L. Polk & Co.'s Wichita City Directory,* 1922–1925 (Wichita, Kans.: R. L. Polk, 1922–1925); *Polk's Wichita City Directory,* 1926–1941 (Kansas City, Mo.: R. L. Polk, 1926–1941); Sedgwick County, Wichita, 1st precinct ward 3, 1925 Kansas Census, volume 203–4, reel 139.

18. *Jinshanke* and *keku,* respectively, in Mandarin.

19. Gas was struck in Augusta, a town near Wichita, in 1903; more gas and also oil was discovered in the same area in 1914, and in 1915, El Dorado tapped into an oil bonanza that by 1918 placed it as a leading oil field in the United States.

The bonanza turned Wichita into a boomtown. See Craig Miner, *Discovery!: Cycles of Change in the Kansas Oil & Gas Industry, 1860–1987* (Wichita, Kans.: KIOGA, 1987), 118–19, 130–31.

20. An examination of city directories for the 1910s and 1920s revealed that the restaurant was most likely established in 1920 and was initially run by Hung Ling, then owned by Mar Lee Quong. King Mar was not listed as owner or manager until 1929, and then when he was, he remained the owner of it until 1969. Henry Mar, another cousin of See Wing, was listed working at various restaurants, but never at the Pan-American Café. It is possible that he was a "silent" partner in that restaurant. Prior to its establishment, it was a cafeteria and then a restaurant, both owned by Euro-Americans. See *R. L. Polk & Co.'s Wichita City Directory, 1917–1925; Polk's Wichita City Directory, 1926–1945;* "Mar Quits after 51 Years: Pan American to Quit," *Wichita-Eagle and Beacon,* June 28, 1969.

21. The "sojourner hypothesis" was first linked to Chinese immigrants in Paul C. P. Siu's article, "The Sojourner," *American Journal of Sociology* 58 (July 1952): 34–43. Though often associated with Chinese immigrants, European and other Asian immigration patterns also witnessed the same phenomenon. This sojourning experience suggests that some immigrants were motivated by the desire for economic betterment, rather than a desperate flight from destitution and social misery. See Franklin Ng, "The Sojourner, Return Migration, and Immigration History," in *Chinese America: History and Perspectives 1987* (San Francisco: Chinese Historical Society of America, 1987), 53–71.

22. Early Chinese immigrants often pooled their resources—typically with those who were members of their extended family or at least belonged to the same ancestral village—to establish business ventures. Some of these partnerships, however, were duplicitous; some Chinese immigrants paid mercantile establishments to list them as partners so as to attain the status of the "merchant," thus enabling them to gain entry into the United States. For one such account, see Bruce Edward Hall, *Tea That Burns: A Family Memoir of Chinatown* (New York: Free Press, 1998), 98–99. Because Wong's real father, See Wing, entered the country as a paper son of a merchant, it is unlikely that he became the owner of a restaurant in order to gain entry. His involvement in a business run by relatives, however, suggests that kinship ties were critical in finding jobs and establishing small businesses in America, which in turn led to clustering of clans and kinfolk in the same occupations. See Paul C. P. Siu, *The Chinese Laundryman: A Study of Social Isolation* (New York: New York University Press, 1987), 77–82; Hsu, *Dreaming of Gold, Dreaming of Home,* 60–61. How kinship ties shaped occupations among Chinese Wichitans is suggested

by the preponderance of Mars—See Wing's true surname—in Wichita for the period 1920 to 1939, and all Mars had occupations tied to the restaurant industry. See *R. L. Polk & Co.'s Wichita City Directory*, 1920–1925; *Polk's Wichita City Directory*, 1926–1939.

23. A total of thirteen Chinese American–owned or –managed restaurants existed between 1920 and 1941. They were the King Fong Café, Mandarin Inn, Oriental Café, Sunlight Café, Nanking Café, Air Capitol Café, Joy Café, Grand Café, Legion Café, Grand Café, Crystal Café, Shanghai Gardens, Fairland Café, Pan-American Café, and Holly Café. Some of these, as Wong indicated, changed owners over the years, and as such underwent name changes. For example, the Legion Café at 110 West Douglas became the Crystal Café in 1931. The period when Wichita had the largest number of such establishments—namely, six—operating at the same time on different premises was between 1929 and 1931. See Note 22.

24. Two restaurants—the Air Capital Café (later Nanking Café) and Joy Café—were about two blocks east of this area. See Note 23.

25. In 1931 seven establishments were in operation, but by 1939, only three still ran as restaurants. See Note 23.

26. During World War II, Wichita became a major defense production center. The aviation industry as a whole received multimillion-dollar production contracts and significant loans from the federal government to expand their plants. Jobs opened up, and the Wichita population grew dramatically from 114,966 to almost 190,000 in 1943. In 1943, 50 percent of Wichitans relied on the aviation industry for their livelihoods, up from just 3 percent in 1939. See Craig Miner, *Wichita, the Magic City: An Illustrated History* (Wichita, Kans.: Wichita–Sedgwick County Historical Museum Association, 1988), 185, 188; Craig Miner, *Kansas: The History of the Sunflower State, 1854–2000* (Lawrence: University Press of Kansas, 2003), 314.

27. From 1941 until 1943, contrary to what Wong claimed, at least four such cafés existed. Besides the Fairland, Holly, and the Pan-American, a Wing Lee Café (formerly the Grand Café) ran from 1940 to 1943. The Wing Lee Café was on 511 East Douglas Avenue. See *Polk's Wichita City Directory*, 1940–1943. Only street directories were published in 1944 and 1945, owing to wartime shortages; Wing Lee Café is not listed in either one of them. See *McGuin's Numerical Street Directory, 1944–1946* (Wichita, Kans.: McGuin Publishing, 1944–1946).

28. The economy in Wichita did contract as thousands lost their jobs, and wartime housing projects were abandoned. However, rapid depopulation in the city did not take place because cautious optimism held out. See Miner, *Magic City*, 192.

29. The Pan-American Café was the longest continuously running Chinese-owned restaurant in Wichita. When it closed, it had been in operation for forty-nine years. See "Mar Quits after 51 Years," *Wichita-Eagle and Beacon*. In this article, King Mar, the manager and one of the five owners, cited the need to take his retirement, plus high overhead costs, as the reasons for the restaurant's closure.

30. As explained in Note 10, the wife of See Wing's paper father could immigrate as part of the exempt classes. Wayne Wong's mother, however, was the wife of a son of a merchant, and technically did not qualify for this right, which explains why Wong's family endured the phenomenon of a "split household" or trans-Pacific family. Other factors might also have played a role in shaping such a phenomenon, such as the Chinese practice of sojourning, traditional gender roles that circumscribed women's mobility, and the fear of racial hostility in America. From 1890 to 1940, one study estimated that two-fifths of Chinese American men were married and lived apart from their wives and children. See Zhao, *Remaking Chinese America* 13; Hsu, *Dreaming of Gold, Dreaming of Home,* 99.

31. Three types of Chinese families existed: the small or conjugal family that was made up of at most two generations; the large or joint family, where multiple generations inhabited one common dwelling; and the stem family of parents, unmarried children, and one married son with his wife and children under one household. See Eastman, *Family, Fields, and Ancestors,* 16. By the time Wong was born, the family organization was the small or conjugal family.

32. Separated wives were also known as *jinsaanpo* (Cantonese *gamsaanpo*) who, in the absence of their husbands, had to shoulder far more responsibilities than women who did not marry a Gold Mountain emigrant. Unlike Wong Sen Kew, some women had to become breadwinners of the family, whenever their spouses defaulted on remittances. See Zhao, *Remaking Chinese America,* 41.

33. Such gossip was part of the larger effort of villagers to maintain the moral code, and in so doing ensured that these separated, Gold Mountain families endured as entities. See Hsu, *Dreaming of Gold, Dreaming of Home,* 104–7.

34. The Chinese Exclusion Act of 1882 suspended the immigration of laborers to the United States for ten years. The suspension was extended for another ten years, and in 1902 for another ten. In 1904, Congress made it indefinite. This law and other related legislation were not repealed until 1943.

35. The Chinese Exclusion Act of 1882 and its subsequent related legislation did not enact job discrimination or mandate the establishment of segregated schools for Chinese pupils. However, scholars agree that the legislation, by ex-

cluding immigrants solely on the basis of their race and nationality, sanctioned discrimination in other areas of life. See Charles J. McClain Jr., *In Search of Equality: The Chinese Struggle against Discrimination in Nineteenth-Century America* (Berkeley: University of California Press, 1994).

36. Victor Jew estimated that there were ninety-one instances of anti-Chinese violence during the 1880s, with seventy-one occurring between 1885 and 1886 alone. See Victor Jew, "Exploring New Frontiers in Chinese American History: The Anti-Chinese Riot in Milwaukee, 1889," in *The Chinese in America: A History from Gold Mountain to the New Millennium,* ed. Susie Lan Cassel (Walnut Creek, Calif.: Altamira Press, 2002), 79.

37. In two separate cases decided in 1884, the courts ruled that Chinese wives of domiciled laborers were also laborers because their status was derived from their husbands. Those wives who did not possess the requisite documentation to ascertain that they had domiciled in the United States were deemed inadmissible given the nature of the Chinese Exclusion Act of 1882. Sucheng Chan, "The Exclusion of Chinese Women, 1870–1943," in *Entry Denied: Exclusion and the Chinese Community in America, 1882–1943,* ed. Sucheng Chan (Philadelphia: Temple University Press, 1991), 110–12.

38. The U.S. Immigration and Naturalization Service (INS) estimated that the 30,460 Chinese whose claims to American citizenship were revealed as fraudulent between 1957 and 1965 made up 25.8 percent of the total Chinese population in 1950. See Mae M. Ngai, "Legacies of Exclusion: Illegal Chinese Immigration during the Cold War Years," *Journal of American Ethnic History* 18 (Fall 1998): 28. See also Mae M. Ngai, *Impossible Subjects: Illegal Aliens and the Making of Modern America* (Princeton, N.J.: Princeton University Press, 2004), 202–24.

39. To circumvent the restrictive immigration laws, some Chinese immigrants crossed either the Canadian or Mexican border to enter the United States. It was possible to do so because no border patrol existed until 1924. Mexico for its part did not prohibit the entry of Chinese laborers until 1921. Illegal border entry, however, did not provide immigrants with the certificates of identity or residency required to avoid being deported in the event they were arrested by immigration authorities. See Erika Lee, "At America's Gates: Chinese Immigration During the Exclusion Era, 1882–1943" (Ph.D. diss., University of California, Berkeley, 1998), 238–45; Hsu, *Dreaming of Gold, Dreaming of Home,* 72; see also Erika Lee, *At America's Gates: Chinese Immigration During the Exclusion Era, 1882–1943* (Chapel Hill: University of North Carolina Press, 2003), 179–87.

40. From 1892 onward, immigration officials did try to force Chinese who claimed citizenry to prove their claim by evidence other than Chinese testimony. Though this regulation led to the denial of entry for many Chinese, they were admitted by judges in the federal district system. Sometime in 1895 immigration officials deemed this requirement overly harsh, and by 1902, the admission of Chinese as citizens based solely on Chinese testimony was fairly common. See Lee, *At America's Gates,* 260.

41. The status of native born undoubtedly placed both Mars in more advantageous positions. As native borns, they would not be subjected to the rigorous system that forced merchants to maintain their mercantile establishments or risk being deported from the country, and not forced to provide detailed information about their business, families in China and the United States, and testimonies from non-Chinese witnesses. Such onerous paperwork was repeated during each trip abroad. See McClain, *In Search of Equality,* 180; Lee, *At America's Gates,* 202–3.

42. Wong Wing Lock's departure from the United States was on January 30, 1912. See entry no. 1336, January 30, 1912, Records of Natives [United States–born Chinese Americans] Departing, 1909–1913, unnumbered microfilm, National Archives—Pacific Sierra Region, San Bruno, Calif.

43. Because Wing Lock left for China in early 1912, Hung Doon must have been born in 1912, rather than 1911. See also Wong Doon You, case no. 29325/7-6, General Index to Immigration Case Files, c. 1910–1979, unnumbered microfilm, National Archives—Pacific Sierra Region, San Bruno, Calif. No Henry Mar or Mar Jill Jing was found in this document.

44. Wong Hung Doon also went by the name of Wong Doon You. On his certificate of identity issued to all newly arriving bona fide Chinese immigrants, he was identified as a student in San Francisco and was admitted on August 20, 1926, and not in 1923. See Wong Doon You, certificate of identity, Certificates of Identity for Chinese Residents, 1909–c. 1946, National Archives—Pacific Sierra Region, San Bruno, Calif.

45. This entry was actually July 4, 1930. See Wong Wing Lock, case no. 293235/7-5, General Index to Immigration Case Files.

46. By the early twentieth century, Chinese Americans, such as Wong Wing Lock and Henry Mar, discovered that U.S. laws granted derivative or statutory U.S. citizenship to children of native-born citizen fathers (but not mothers). U.S. citizens of Chinese ancestry exploited this by reporting the birth of their children to the authorities in order to create "slots" that could be sold to those who were not their sons. Note that in both Henry Mar's and Wing Lock's cases, the immigration of boys was privileged over the girls, echoing a larger pattern

in the Chinese community. The reasons for this pattern included patriarchal cultural values, the Chinese belief that boys stood a better chance of securing a living in America, and perhaps more important, unlike boys, girls who were citizens could never grant their children derivative citizenship. See Zhao, *Remaking Chinese America,* 29, 33, 36.

47. The deposition books mentioned here were more commonly called "coaching books" or "coaching papers." The books contained all the details of the immigrants' assumed identities that the immigration officials would probably cover during the immigration-clearance process. Typically, the books also offered the questions immigration officials might pose to new arrivals. The mere possession of papers or documents attesting to one's assumed identity was insufficient to convince immigration officials of one's right to land; the officials knew of the pervasiveness of the "paper son" scheme. The information in these books or papers sometimes was compiled by the immigrants themselves, and at other times by professional "coaching paper" writers. See Lee, *At America's Gates,* 196–98.

48. Owing to the exacting nature of the coaching papers, immigrants such as Wayne Wong spent considerable time studying them. Another immigrant recalled, "It took me quite a few months to prepare myself, I get the book from my uncle about six months ahead. My duty was just forget about everything, just memorize the book. I have total of eighty something names I have to remember!" Quoted in Lee, *At America's Gates,* 291.

49. This decision of Sen Kew to uproot herself and her children to Guangzhou and live with members of her natal family, though a break with the patrilocal nature of Chinese traditional families, was not unique. There were instances of *jinshaanpo* who forged close ties to their natal families either to gain or offer emotional and material support in an era when families in China were denied the assistance of emigrated male members. See Sandra M. J. Wong, "For the Sake of Kinship: The Overseas Chinese Family" (Ph.D. diss., Stanford University, 1987), 41–46.

50. See Wing's decision to purchase the "native-born" identity of Moy Jing's son for Wayne Wong was in step with the overall trend after 1920 whereby the number of Chinese entering the United States as foreign-born children of citizens clearly outpaced that of those entering as "raw natives" (i.e., those who claimed to be native-born citizens returning to the country since their recent departures). See Wing's decision here also hints that another factor might have been involved: after *Chin Yow v United States* (1928), the grandchildren of Chinese persons born in the United States—which is exactly what Wong's male children would be, in accordance with his assumed identity—were ad-

mitted lawfully, though not considered citizens of the United States. See Lee, *At America's Gates*, 277.

51. The cost here for the assumed identity was not unusually high. Most of the paperwork during this interwar period cost anywhere between $1,000 and $3,000. See Hsu, *Dreaming of Gold, Dreaming of Home*, 72; Lee, *At America's Gates*, 284.

52. *Meiguo* in Mandarin.

53. The dependency of Taishanese on their clanspeople overseas for monetary support is discussed in Hsu, *Dreaming of Gold, Dreaming of Home*, 40–49.

54. In recent years, Chinese American historians have argued that some immigrants—and Wayne Wong could be included in this group—were not unworldly victims of Western capitalism who were pushed out of China, but rather people who had experienced modernity and had been exposed to Western civilization. They made the decision to immigrate to maintain and improve their status and lifestyle. See Yong Chen, "Internal Origins to Chinese Immigration Reconsidered," *Western Historical Quarterly* 25 (Winter 1997): 538–41, 545–46; Haiming Liu, "The Social Origins of Early Chinese Immigrants: A Revisionist Perspective," in *The Chinese in America: A History from Gold Mountain to the New Millennium*, ed. Susie Lan Cassel (Walnut Creek, Calif.: Altamira Press, 2002), 21–36.

55. Chinese immigrants in the early twentieth century who planned to enter the United States could also disembark at Vancouver, British Columbia, and then board the Canadian-Pacific Railroad to one of four border crossings: Sumas, Washington; Portal, North Dakota; Richford, Vermont; or Malone, New York. Those who arrived by sea in New York were processed at Ellis Island. See Benson Tong, *The Chinese Americans*, 2d ed. (Boulder: University Press of Colorado, 2003), 30.

56. In keeping the deposition or coaching book, Wong's actions departed from those of most immigrants, who typically threw it overboard or destroyed it as the ship approached the American shores. See Him Mark Lai, Genny Lim, and Judy Yung, *Island: Poetry and History of Chinese Immigrants on Angel Island, 1910–1940* (Seattle: University of Washington Press, 1991), 20.

57. The date of his arrival was December 1, 1935, but he was not officially processed by the immigration authorities until December 18. See Wong Hung Yin, case no. 7030/8234, General Index to Immigration Case files, c. 1910–1979, National Archives—Pacific Sierra Region, San Bruno, Calif. The only "alien" on that *Princess of Alice* voyage was Frank Lung, a nineteen-year-old Chinese student. Wong undoubtedly entered the country as the son of a native born. See ticket no. 23993/1, *Inbound Passenger Manifests and Crew Lists (Prior to*

12/1/54), October 17, 1935–December, 30, 1935, M 1383, reel 210, National Archives and Record Services, Washington, D.C.

58. At the Angel Island Immigration Station on San Francisco Bay, all arriving Chinese immigrants had to first undergo a rigorous health inspection designed to thwart the spread of contagious infections. Racial assumptions regarding Asian susceptibility to diseases undergirded some of those examinations. By the 1910s, half of the deported arrivals were turned away because of medical reasons. See Nayan Shah, *Contagious Divides: Epidemics and Race in San Francisco's Chinatown* (Berkeley: University of California Press, 2001), 179–202.

59. At Angel Island, a few fortunate immigrants did have their applications to land processed within a week, but most took longer. A backlog of cases often delayed the first interrogations by several weeks. Those who had their applications rejected could appeal to the commissioner of immigration in Washington, D.C. Such appeals could prolong the detainment from six months to a year. See Judy Yung, *Unbound Feet: A Social History of Chinese Women in San Francisco* (Berkeley: University of California Press, 1996), 66; Him Mark Lai, "Island of Immortals: Chinese Immigrants and the Angel Island Station," *California History* 57 (Spring 1978): 98.

60. Missionaries, in an attempt to proselytize, also visited Angel Island detainees, primarily to teach needlework, offer English lessons, and organize holiday programs. See Yung, *Unbound Feet,* 67.

61. Unlike European immigrants processed at Ellis Island, Chinese immigrants at Angel Island were subjected to, according to one study, from about two hundred to more than one thousand questions. See Wen-Hsien Chen, "Chinese Under Both Exclusion and Immigration Laws" (Ph.D. diss., University of Chicago, 1940), 107.

62. The lack of documentary evidence of births in China forced immigration officials to resort to testimonies as the only way to prove relationships. Officials relied on Hung Doon's testimony to gauge the truthfulness of Wong's identity. In cases involving siblings (or fathers and sons), the level of physical resemblance also played a role in determining the claimed relationship. See Lee, *At America's Gates,* 333–34, 338.

63. Wong's case was probably unique. Some immigrants processed through Angel Island complained that the intensive interrogations sometimes bordered on harassment. Chinese immigrants felt intimidated by the rigorous investigations imposed on them. See Lee, *At America's Gates,* 355–56.

64. Before leaving the immigration detention station, Wong was issued a certificate of identity that proved his legitimate residence in the United States,

and also in his case, as noted in the certificate, his U.S. citizenship by way of being the native son of Wong Wing Lock. Such certificates were also issued to members of the exempt classes. Note that Wong Hung Yin's certificate of identity, similar to what one would find in other certificates, provide detailed "physical marks and peculiarities": "horizontal scar under L [left] side chin; face lightly covered with fine pits; several larger pits between eyes & eyebrows; pin mole R [right] cheek." Such details enabled immigration officials, upon Wong's return to the United States from a visit to China, to check the veracity of the identity of the person appearing before them. Typically, those who possessed such certificates could bypass detainment on Angel Island. The certificate also provided his age, height, and occupation, which was listed as "student" residing in Chicago. Officially, Wong was admitted into the United States on January 6, 1936. See Wong Hung Yin, certificate of identity, Certificates of Identity for Chinese Residents, 1909–c. 1946.

Chapter 2: Life in Wichita, 1936–42

1. Wichita city directories from 1936 to 1940 do not list Wayne Wong, either his real or paper name. However, both the 1938 and 1940 issues do list a "Wong, Wing" identified as a student living at the address of the restaurant. When questioned, Wayne Wong admitted using Wing as his personal name in combination with Wong. The 1941 issue does list "Wong, Wayne" as a helper at the restaurant. See *Polk's Wichita City Directory, 1936–1941* (Kansas City, Mo.: R. L. Polk, 1936–1941).

2. It is uncertain why the owners of the restaurant did not purchase the building; perhaps their sojourner status made it unwise to do so. According to county records, the building and lot were owned by various individuals from 1917 to 1944, all of whom were European Americans. See Transfer Record A-A-2 Lots, Sedgwick County, p. 57, County Clerk Real Estate Records, Sedgwick County, Kansas. The Lassen Hotel was built in 1918, and in the 1980s was converted into an office building. See *Discover Historic Wichita! A Listing of Wichita's Registered Historic Landmarks & Districts* (Wichita, Kans.: Historic Preservation Office, Metropolitan Area Planning Department, Wichita, 1997), 23–24.

3. An examination of the Sanborn Fire Insurance Map for 1935 for this locale supports this description. A "wall paper, paints, & oils" store was adjacent to the Pan-American Café. On the other side of the restaurant was a "whole electrical appliances" establishment. The restaurant itself was a mix of "hollow concrete or cement block" and "brick" construction with wired-glass skylight. The establishment featured window openings on the first floor, but none on

the other two. The entire restaurant actually took up two numbers, i.e., 150 and 152. See *Sanborn Fire Insurance Maps of Wichita: 1935* (New York: Sanborn Map Publishing, 1937).

4. A close examination of photographs of the restaurant also reveals ceiling fans, art deco light fixtures, oil paintings on the walls, and wallpaper above wooden paneling on the walls. See photograph album, Wayne Wong personal papers.

5. See Note 22 for the clustering of kinfolk or clans in the same occupations.

6. A few of the Pan-American Café workers did not live above the restaurant. For example, Gee Mar, who was most likely Wong's real father, changed residence from 150 North Market (the address of the restaurant) sometime between 1925 and 1929 to 154-1/2 North Market Street. See the 1925 Kansas Census, 1st precinct ward 3, vols. 203 and 204, Sedgwick County, Wichita, Reel 139; *Polk's Wichita Directory,* 1929.

7. Changes in immigration laws after the war enabled Chinese American veterans to bring "war brides" and existing wives to the United States. See the introductory essay.

8. No published study exists currently on the work culture of Chinese restaurant workers during the exclusion era. A landmark study on the other equally ubiquitous occupation for Chinese during this era, the laundryman, is Siu, *Chinese Laundryman.*

9. Wichita's population in 1930, according to the U.S. Bureau of Census, was 119,174. See Miner, *Magic City,* 179. No figure exists for the city's Chinese population. Because the state's Chinese population was sixty, and assuming that all of the Chinese lived in urban areas, Wong's estimate is probably close to being accurate. See Bureau of the Census, *1980 Census of Population, vol. 1 Characteristics of the Population Part 18 Kansas* (Washington, D.C., 1982), 22.

10. Wing Sen is listed in the 1938 Wichita City Directory, but not in any other directory for the other years of that decade. His was one of the few names unidentified by nature of occupation. See *Polk's Wichita City Directory,* 1930–1940.

11. A search of local archives in Wichita for school yearbooks or other related records was fruitless. Nevertheless, two newspaper articles reported of five students of Chinese descent in that school in 1935, a number that increased to seven in 1940. See "Chinese Are Increasing in Spite of Law," *Wichita Eagle,* November 19, 1935; "Wichita Educator Is Solving Unusual Problem," *Wichita Eagle,* February 25, 1940.

12. The Chinese students at Carleton, with the exception of Wong, were the

subject of a newspaper article. See "Chinese Are Increasing in Spite of Law," *Wichita Eagle.*

13. The only report card that Wong retained is his ninth grade one that shows he earned A's in Math, Spelling, English, Social Studies, Typing, and Gym. The teachers also gave him A's for courtesy, dependability, initiative, cooperation, and industry. Ninth grade report card, Central Intermediate School, 1941, Wayne Wong personal papers.

14. Church, peers, and popular culture also Americanized second-generation Chinese American youngsters, which in turn led them to self-identify as "Americans." See Sucheng Chan, "Race, Ethnic Culture, and Gender in the Construction of Identities among Second-Generation Chinese Americans, 1880s to 1930s," in *Claiming America: Constructing Chinese American Identities During the Exclusion Era,* ed. K. Scott Wong and Sucheng Chan (Philadelphia: Temple University Press, 1998), 128, 157. To some extent, Wong also experienced this Americanization.

15. Wayne Wong's racially mixed school, though still predominantly white, was a departure from the norm. Separate educational facilities for black and white children in Wichita primary grades was mandated through the action of the state legislature in 1909 and 1912, marking the first year of segregation in Wichita's primary schools. See Miner, *Kansas,* 256. Black students who lived in white districts were transported to segregated schools. *De jure* segregation in education in Wichita ended in 1952, following repeated appeals of African American activists and parents to the local board of education. See Gretchen Cassel Eick, *Dissent in Wichita: The Civil Rights Movement in the Midwest, 1954–1972* (Urbana: University of Illinois Press, 2001), 18, 29–31.

16. A photograph taken in 1939 in a Wichita photo studio shows Wayne Wong and eight other Chinese male youngsters, which Wong claims was the total number of youngsters in Wichita at that time. See photo album, Wayne Wong personal papers.

17. Wichita theaters were segregated by race, and as late as the 1960s, blacks were still being shunted to the back of theaters. See Miner, *Magic City,* 205.

18. In 1929, Wichita had six Chinese-owned restaurants but ten years later, only three remained. See *Polk's Wichita City Directory,* 1929–1939.

19. Wichita did suffer the impact of the Great Depression. The city government's budget was dramatically reduced and salaries were cut, but compared to some cities, Wichita weathered it better owing in part to the federal largesse that arrived as part of the New Deal programs. See Miner, *Magic City,* 177–80.

20. Sociologist Paul C. P. Siu, in his study conducted in the late 1930s in Chicago, observed that "boys of adolescent age are seen everywhere in Chi-

nese laundries." These boys immigrated to join fathers, brothers, uncles, or grandfathers. See Siu, *Chinese Laundryman,* 78.

21. This description of the initial reaction of the people at the restaurant echoes that of most Americans about that turning point. See Ronald Takaki, *Double Victory: A Multicultural History of America in World War II* (Boston: Little, Brown, 2000), 8–14.

22. Racial lumping threw Chinese and Japanese together, while ethnic profiling led some whites to ignore the difference between Japanese nationals who aided Japan's imperialist goals and Americans of Japanese and Chinese ancestry. Americans of Chinese (and Japanese) descent became targets of anti-Japanese nativism, even though official government propaganda and the media differentiated between the two Asian groups, portraying the Chinese as U.S. allies and Japanese the enemy. See Iris Chang, *The Chinese in America: A Narrative History* (New York: Viking, 2003), 225.

Chapter 3: In the Army

1. A search of local newspapers for 1941 using incomplete indexes revealed no such parade. There was one major parade in 1942 that was part of the Memorial Day celebration that also featured military vehicles, veterans' organizations, and companies of soldiers. See "To Honor Memory of Heroes of All Wars Here Today," *Wichita Eagle,* May 30, 1942.

2. From New York to San Francisco, Chinese Americans in small and large cities participated in various parades, raised funds for the Red Cross, volunteered for civil defense work, and rationed necessities as they responded to the rallying cry for all Americans to support the war effort. Chinese Americans deemed the fight against fascism as also the fight to save China, which in turn would improve their subordinated status in the United States. See K. Scott Wong, "War Comes to Chinatown: Social Transformation and the Chinese of California," in *The Way We Really Were: The Golden State in the Second Great War,* ed. Roger Lotchin (Urbana: University of Illinois Press, 2000), 178–81.

3. The Selective Service and Training Act that instituted the peacetime draft was signed into law by President Franklin D. Roosevelt on September 16, 1940. The law mandated that inductees would serve for twelve months (extended in 1941 through another law for an additional eighteen months). Some 16.4 million American males between the ages of twenty-one and thirty-five registered for the draft in early October 1940. The draft came in the wake of the fall of France into the hands of Germany in June 1940, and marked the end of the isolationist tradition in the United States. After Pearl Harbor, the draft

was extended to include men up to the age of forty-five. In 1942 those between ages eighteen and twenty were required to register and be liable for military service. By the end of the war years, forty-five million men were registered and ten million drafted into the war. See J. Garry Clifford and Samuel R. Spencer Jr., *The First Peacetime Draft* (Lawrence: University Press of Kansas, 1986), 3, 6, 231; Lewis B. Hershey, *Selective Service in Wartime: Second Report of the Director of Selective Service, 1941–1942* (Washington, D.C.: Government Printing Office, 1943), 5, 11, 55.

4. Clergy (including students and brothers), foreign diplomatic personnel, high officials of the government, conscientious objectors, as well as those the president deemed necessary to the "maintenance of the national health, safety, or interest" were offered deferment of service. See Clifford and Spencer, *First Peacetime Draft*, 42, 76, 140–41. Those in classification IV-F also included those deemed mentally and morally unfit. See Hershey, *Selective Service in Wartime*, 225.

5. Wong is probably referring to the impending liability of men between ages eighteen and twenty, rather than eighteen and twenty-five, for military service, which was enacted by law in November 1942. See Hershey, *Selective Service in Wartime*, 11.

6. The actual name of the school was National Defense Training School. Wong's education there lasted seven months. See Yin Hung Wong, separation qualification record, Wayne Wong personal papers.

7. See Yin Hung Wong, Enlisted Record and Report of Separation, December 21, 1945, Wayne Wong personal papers.

8. Since the Marco Polo Bridge Incident of July 1937 that initiated the Sino-Japanese War, the Japanese by early 1939 had captured virtually all of the major cities, as well as south China seaports. After 1939 the war in China entered into a long stalemate, punctuated by occasional battles. See Edward L. Dreyer, *China at War, 1901–1949* (London: Longman, 1995), 260–61.

9. A thorough search of Wichita city directories for 1941 to 1943 reveal no such names in them. However, the directories are known to be incomplete.

10. Wong is most likely alluding to the shortage of meat because of ration restrictions that forced some downtown restaurants during wartime to close one day a week from 1943 onward. See "Will Close Cafes One Day Each Week to Conserve Meat," *Wichita Eagle*, April 8, 1943.

11. Wong's position in the Enlisted Reserve Corps was "mechanic learner (radio)," which midway through the training in Kansas City became "junior repairman trainee (radio)." See Cecil F. McGee to Wayne H. Wong, November 24, 1942, SPKGW 230.02 (M), U.S. War Department; Wayne H. Wong,

vocational training record card, July 14, 1943, copies in Wayne Wong personal papers.

12. The camp had the capacity to house 8,742 enlisted men and 347 officers on 3,563 acres. See Shelby L. Stanton, *Order of Battle, U.S. Army, World War II* (Novato, Calif.: Presidio Press, 1984), 600.

13. Chinese American women in California also established separate social spaces similar to USO clubs to welcome Chinese servicemen who felt unwelcome in the latter establishments. See Wong, "War Comes to Chinatown," 179.

14. In 1940 there were a total of 30,046 Chinese in that city, compared to the total Chinese population in the United States, which was 77,504. See Judy Yung, *Unbound Feet: A Social History of Chinese Women in San Francisco* (Berkeley: University of California Press, 1995), 293, 296.

15. The course lasted nine weeks and ended in early November 1943. See Wong, separation qualification record.

16. Chinese American soldiers recruited into the segregated units came from almost all the states of the Union. See Peter Phan, "Familiar Strangers: The Fourteenth Air Service Group Case Study of Chinese American Identity During World War II," in *Chinese America: History and Perspectives 1993* (San Francisco: Chinese Historical Society of America, 1993), 82.

17. Camp Crowder was located in Neosho, Missouri, and was designated the Signal Corps Training Center. It had the capacity to house 40,642 enlisted men and 1,988 officers on a total acreage of 43,007. See Stanton, *Order of Battle,* 508.

18. The "Flying Tigers" was the popular name of the American Volunteer Group led by General Claire Lee Chennault that was recruited in the summer of 1941 to work for the Chinese Air Force, and the group began its operations in December of that year. It is credited by one writer as having downed almost three hundred Japanese planes, while its own loss was eighty-six planes. In 1943 the American Volunteer Group became the nucleus of the Fourteenth Air Force. See Daniel Ford, *Flying Tigers: Claire Chennault and the American Volunteer Group* (Washington, D.C.: Smithsonian Institution Press, 1991), 369, 371.

19. The other nine units were the 407th Air Service Squadron, 555th Air Service Squadron, 1077th Quartermaster Company, 1157th Signal Company, 1544th Ordnance Company, 1545th Ordnance Company, 2121st Quartermaster Trucking Company, 2122d Quartermaster Trucking Company, and a headquarters squadron. See Phan, "Familiar Strangers," 81. The China-Burma-India theater of operations covered more than four thousand miles, from Mongolia, across central China, over the Himalayas, and into India to Ceylon (now Sri Lanka).

In 1944 the theater was split in two: the China theater and the India-Burma theater. See Don Moser and the editors of Time-Life Books, *China-Burma-India* (Alexandria, Va.: Time-Life Books, 1978), 18–20.

20. These men might have been reassigned to the trucking companies (2121st and 2122d), which apparently took in recruits with limited English skills. See Christina M. Lim and Sheldon H. Lim, "In the Shadow of the Tiger: The 407th Air Service Squadron, Fourteenth Air Force, CBI, World War II," in *Chinese America: History and Perspectives* (San Francisco: Chinese Historical Society, 1993), 29.

21. In other units, a language barrier existed between the Chinese American enlistees. Some spoke very little Chinese, while others spoke very little English. See Phan, "Familiar Strangers," 82.

22. As suggested a number of times in this autobiography, Wong's repeated references to Chinese food and his interest in seeking out such cuisine shows one way of maintaining one's ethnic identity, as well as being a statement of cultural cohesion. See similar examples of other Chinese servicemen in ibid., 93–95.

23. Wong's money was used to purchase the Nationalist government's Thrift and Reconstruction Savings Accounts through the auspices of the Bank of China. See Milton C. Lee to Yin Hung Wong, June 18, 1943, letter, copy in Wayne Wong personal papers.

24. Chinese American women who served in the armed services also complained that their uniforms did not fit; Marjorie Lee, "Coming of Age: Chinese American Women Doing Their Part," in *Duty and Honor: A Tribute to Chinese American World War II Veterans of Southern California*, ed. Marjorie Lee (Los Angeles: Chinese Historical Society of Southern California, 1998), 54–55.

25. Toishan is the Cantonese name for Taishan.

26. The tragedy of the SS *Jean Nicolet* is recounted in Oliver Borlaug, ed., *History of the 14th Air Service Group and the 987th Signal Group* (n.p.: BHG, Inc., Garrison, 1995), 46.

27. The camp was the main staging area for the CBI theater. Lim and Lim, "In the Shadow of the Tiger," 40.

28. Wong's observations were echoed by other Chinese servicemen who visited that city. See ibid.

29. The "Hump" refers to a five-hundred-mile air route that stretched from bases in Assam province, India, to Kunming, China. This was a difficult air route owing to the mountain range it passed over, poor weather conditions, and the threat of enemy planes; Moser et al., *China-Burma-India*, 80. The Hump replaced the earlier "Burma Road," a circuitous land route of two

thousand miles over difficult terrain from the Burmese port of Rangoon to the Nationalist capital of Chongqing, which the Japanese forces took partial control of in 1942.

30. For more on leisure in Kunming, see Lim and Lim, "In the Shadow of the Tiger," 48–49.

31. During the war years, the Nationalist government based in Chongqing, Sichuan province, resorted to inflationary finance to make up the shortfall in public revenues. Expanded note issues led to skyrocketing price levels, a falling exchange rate, and high interest rates. See Suzanne Pepper, *Civil War in China: The Political Struggle, 1945–1949,* 2d ed. (Lanham, Md.: Rowman & Littlefield, 1999), 95.

32. Until March 9, 1945, when Japanese forces disarmed the French and disbanded the French colonial government of Indochina, Japan officially did not rule Indochina; however, French economic and political concessions to Japan were sufficient to meet its imperialistic designs in that region. See Donald Lancaster, *The Emancipation of French Indochina* (London: Oxford University Press, 1961), 96.

33. American infantry, artillery, veterinary, engineering, medical, and air personnel were also attached to Chinese armies and divisions. Overall, such personnel were called the Y-Force Operations Staff and were assigned to help Chinese forces clear the Japanese from the Chinese end of the Burma Road. See Charles F. Romanus and Riley Sunderland, *Time Runs Out in CBI* (Washington, D.C.: Office of the Chief of Military History, Department of the Army, 1959), 28.

34. Because the Chinese Nationalist government backed the Vietnamese Nationalist coalition of Dong Minh Hoi, its military forces offered assistance to the latter's advance into Indochina before Japan's August surrender. Chinese forces, however, did not occupy northern Indochina until after the surrender. See King C. Chen, *Vietnam and China, 1938–1954* (Princeton, N.J.: Princeton University Press, 1969), 61–71, 104–5, 115.

35. The supply woes were compounded by the fact that the CBI theater was "a war fought at the end of the longest supply line in the world." Furthermore, with the Allies more interested in defeating Germany first before turning their attention to Japan, the CBI became the dumping ground for inferior equipment and supplies. See Charles F. Romanus and Riley Sunderland, *Stillwell's Command Problems* (Washington, D.C.: Office of the Chief of Military History, Department of the Army, 1956), 288–93; quote in Lim and Lim, "In the Shadow of the Tiger," 42.

36. In January 1943 Lieutenant General Joseph W. Stillwell, the chief of staff

of the China-Burma-India theater, ordered U.S. instructors to set up training centers for the Chinese Yunnan divisions, also known as the Y-Force, in artillery, infantry, and signal communications in the Kunming and outlying areas. See Charles F. Romanus and Riley Sunderland, *Stillwell's Mission to China* (Washington, D.C.: Office of the Chief of Military History, Department of War, 1952), 195, 292.

37. For accounts of these activities, see also Borlaug, *History of the Fourteenth Air Service Group,* 74.

38. The railroad referred to here is the Yunnan-Indochina Railway that the Japanese occupation of Indochina closed from September 1940 onward. Romanus and Sunderland, *Stillwell's Mission to China,* 8.

39. The exigencies of waging a war prevented most Chinese American servicemen from visiting their relatives in China; some, however, were fortunate that at the end of the war the authorities made provisions for them to visit Guangdong, the ancestral origins of most of them. See Lim and Lim, "In the Shadow of the Tiger," 61.

40. Chinese American personnel based in China complained that the mail took far too long to arrive—typically it took up to nine weeks. See Borlaug, *History of the 14th Air Service Group,* 24.

41. Similar celebrations also took place in other Chinese American units stationed in China. See Lim and Lim, "In the Shadow of the Tiger," 60.

42. Chiang Kai-shek as commander in chief of the China theater was given the right to designate the Chinese military officers to whom the commanders of Japanese formations should surrender. See Dreyer, *China at War,* 306.

43. Japanese units assembled in northern Indochina surrendered to General Lu Han, the commander of the 1st Front Army, in Hanoi. Japanese units in southern China surrendered in various designated locations. See Hsu Long-hsuen and Chang Ming-kai, comp., *History of the Sino-Japanese War (1937–1945)* (Taipei: Chung Wu Publishing, 1971), 566–67.

44. After the Japanese surrendered, Chinese, rather than American military forces, occupied northern Indochina. Several American military groups did appear in Hanoi between August and September to facilitate the Chinese occupation. See Chen, *Vietnam and China,* 116–17.

45. This date marked the signing of the formal surrender treaty onboard the USS *Missouri.*

46. The incident described in the next three paragraphs refers to the "Kunming Incident." This event was precipitated by Chiang Kai-shek's efforts to strip Yunnan-based militarist Lung Yun of his military power. The conflict erupted on October 2, 1945, and ended with Lung Yun's surrender on October

5. According to historian Lloyd E. Eastman, the Yunnanese and the central-government troops killed "each other with a vengeance that might better have been saved for the Japanese." See Lloyd E. Eastman, *Seeds of Destruction: Nationalist China in War and Revolution 1937–1949* (Stanford, Calif.: Stanford University Press, 1984), 36–38.

47. Wong ended his wartime service with the rank of staff sergeant. The official date of his honorable discharge was December 21, 1945. See Wong, separation qualification record.

Chapter 4: Finding a War Bride

1. Wong was in the Enlisted Reserve Corps. See Edward F. Witsell to Yin Hung Wong, undated, letter, Adjutant General's Office, U.S. War Department, copy in Wayne Wong personal papers.

2. Because of a Japanese offensive in 1944, some farmers in Guangdong abandoned their fields, and as late as 1946, 30 to 40 percent of the land remained untilled in that province. Economic stagnation, inflationary finance on the part of the Nationalist government, and corruption in officialdom compounded the situation. See Lloyd E. Eastman, *Seeds of Destruction: Nationalist China in War and Revolution 1937–1949* (Stanford, Calif.: Stanford University Press, 1984), 71–73.

3. The GI Bill did *not* give Wong that right. What Wong was alluding to was the 1945 War Brides Act, which allowed spouses and children of U.S. citizens to gain nonquota visas during the next three years. A total of 5,726 Chinese spouses and dependents entered under the 1945 law. See Xiaojian Zhao, *Remaking Chinese America: Immigration, Family, and Community, 1940–1965* (New Brunswick, N.J.: Rutgers University Press, 2002), 39, 80.

4. In the Chinese tradition, an engagement does not exist in the Western sense. Rather, the exchange of gifts here is the first stage of the wedding. See Maurice Freedman, *The Study of Chinese Society: Essays by Maurice Freedman* (Stanford, Calif.: Stanford University Press, 1979), 290.

5. Wong's wedding followed fairly closely the traditional Chinese rituals. For an anthropological discussion, see Freedman, *Study of Chinese Society,* 288–95.

6. During the exclusion era, the legality of traditional Chinese marriage customs became the focus of immigration officials' attempt to deny entry to the wives of Chinese merchants. See Chan, "Exclusion of Chinese Women," 114–18. Wong's second marriage was most likely a response to that recent contested issue.

7. The ship's name was actually SS *General M. C. Meige. General Gordon* was the ship that Wong took to China in 1946. See San Francisco INS file 1300–52832, Records of War Brides with Children, 1946–1948, National Archives—Pacific Sierra Region, San Bruno, Calif.

8. Wong was asked a total of thirty questions that covered three typed pages. See Note 10 for a comparison to the number of questions posed to his wife and the length of her transcript. See San Francisco's INS file 1300–32832, Records of War Brides with Children, 1946–1948, National Archives—Pacific Sierra Region, San Bruno, Calif.

9. By then, the Angel Island Immigration Station was no longer in operation, having shut down in 1940. After the war years, the detention center was at 630 Sansome Street near San Francisco's waterfront. See Him Mark Lai, Genny Lim, and Judy Yung, *Island: Poetry and History of Chinese Immigrants on Angel Island, 1910–1940* (San Francisco: Hoc Doi, 1986), 14. Some of the "old" war brides were most likely long-separated wives who took advantage of the Chinese Alien Wives of American Citizens Act of 1946, which enabled U.S. citizens of Chinese ancestry to sponsor the entry of their spouses outside the national origins quota. See Zhao, *Remaking Chinese America,* 81.

10. Kim Suey's claim of a short interrogation is supported by the length of the typed transcript of the interrogation, which covered only three pages (and twenty-eight questions); in contrast, Chinese immigrants during the exclusion era were subjected to interrogations that covered between twenty and eighty typewritten pages. See Note 9; Chen, "Chinese Under Both Exclusion and Immigration Laws," 107.

11. The detainment was compounded by the fact they were not allowed to see anyone from the outside. Feelings of uncertainty about their future also contributed to the emotional anguish. See Zhao, *Remaking Chinese America,* 86.

12. The chronological sequence of events took a longer time to play out than what is suggested here. The Chinese American community's protest began in the summer of 1948, which led to quicker processing of Chinese immigrants in the following two years. See ibid., 91–92, 153.

13. Hung Doon most likely took advantage of the Chinese Alien Wives of American Citizens Act of 1946 to bring his wife into the country. A total of 2,317 women entered between 1947 and 1950. See Note 9; see also Zhao, *Remaking Chinese America,* 80.

14. In 1936 the San Francisco office of the Bureau of Immigration reported that the 14,276 citizens of Chinese descent who were admitted into the United States in the previous eleven years claimed to have parented 33,611 sons but only 2,813

daughters. See Adam McKeown, "Transnational Chinese Families and Chinese Exclusion, 1875–1943," *Journal of American Ethnic History* 18 (Winter 1999): 84.

15. The San Francisco district office of the Immigration and Naturalization Service, and not Congress, started the Chinese Confession Program. Beginning in 1956 a procedure for an administrative adjustment of status was made available to those who were willing to make a voluntary disclosure of their false status. By confessing, ex–paper sons like Hung Doon could then take advantage of the preference categories for family reunification that first received some emphasis in the 1952 McCarran-Walter Immigration Act, and then was expanded for Chinese Americans via a legislative amendment—PL 86–363—that allowed Chinese relatives of U.S. citizens and permanent residents to enter the United States under nonquota status. See Mae M. Ngai, "Legacies of Exclusion: Illegal Chinese Immigration during the Cold War Years," *Journal of American Ethnic History* 18 (Fall 1978): 21; Christina Lim and Sheldon Lim, "VFW Chinatown Eastbay Post #3956: A Story of the Fight for Non-Quota Immigration in the Postwar Period," *Amerasia Journal* 24, no. 1 (1998): 59–83.

16. The confession program typically involved an interview. See Ngai, "Legacies of Exclusion," 24.

17. The difference between Wong's and Kim Suey's cases was that as a veteran, Wong was entitled to naturalized citizenship as long as he had served in the armed forces for a minimum of ninety days. Kim Suey, however, was eligible for a suspension of deportation and permanent resident status because she had resided in the United States for a minimum of seven years. See Ngai, "Legacies of Exclusion," 21.

18. The 1965 Immigration and Nationality Act (actually amendments to an earlier immigration law) placed a much greater emphasis on family reunification than it did on occupation, and most visas thus were reserved for relatives. See Roger Daniels, "United States Policy Towards Asian Immigrants: Contemporary Developments in Historical Perspective," in *New American Destinies: A Reader in Contemporary Asian and Latino Immigration,* ed. Darrell Y. Hamamoto and Rodolfo D. Torres (New York: Routledge, 1997), 81–82. Kim Suey probably took advantage of this change in the law.

19. Another possible reason for the lack of urgency in reclaiming his family name was that his father, Jee See Wing (alias Mar Tung Jing) and his paper father, Wong Wing Lock, had also confessed. See Wing, for his part, also reclaimed his family name. Therefore, later on, See Wing was able to sponsor the immigration of his wife and children. As such, it was unnecessary for Wong to reclaim his real family name for the purpose of sponsoring the immigration of his family members. For Jee See Wing's case file, see 21226/4-4, Arrival

Investigation Case Files, 1884–1944. Information in this case file suggests that See Wing confessed in 1964, while Wing Lock confessed in 1963, events that clearly follow after Hung Kin's confession.

Chapter 5: Raising a Family in Wichita

1. Craig Miner suggests that the peacetime adjustment in Wichita was "brief and comfortable," i.e., the population size shrunk but only for a short time, wartime production contracted but business optimism held out, and by 1948 the city's economy was on the move again when the local Boeing plant received a large Air Force contract to build the B-47. See Craig Miner, *Wichita, the Magic City: An Illustrated History* (Wichita, Kans.: Wichita–Sedgwick County Historical Museum Assocation, 1988), 192–93.

2. Residential segregation was obvious in Wichita during the 1940s and 1950s. In 1950 only three contiguous census tracts had predominantly minority populations (i.e., 50 percent or more). Most African Americans lived in these three tracts, located north and east of the downtown district. Asians resided primarily in two contiguous tracts west of the downtown district, although the census information included those of Middle Eastern descent. Very few Asians (or African Americans) could be found living in the downtown district, which is where the Wongs were trying to find housing. Ten years later three tracts with 50 percent or more minority populations had grown to seven, but the minority population of the city as a whole remained clustered in the northeast part of the city. In 1962 a local planning commission proclaimed that Wichita was "one of the most tightly segregated cities in the nation in terms of residence." See Gretchen Cassel Eick, *Dissent in Wichita: The Civil Rights Movement in the Midwest, 1954–1972* (Urbana: University of Illinois Press, 2001), 22; Donald O. Cowgill, *A Pictorial Analysis of Wichita* (Wichita, Kans.: Community Planning Council and Wichita State University, 1954), 26–27, 30–31.

3. A search for the 1958 article in the local newspapers was fruitless.

4. The first time the Wongs are listed in the city directory under this address is 1954. See *Polk's Wichita City Directory*, 1954.

5. The Korean War did give a boost to the local economy, particularly the aviation industry, but some of that growth was already taking place before the war. See Miner, *Magic City*, 193.

6. Restrictive covenants typically committed homeowners not to sell property to Jews or blacks. Either home owners signed collective agreements or it was a separate document that the real estate company provided, and was signed as part of the title deed.

7. Wong clearly received his diploma by mail and was not part of the graduation ceremony because he was not on North High School's May 1952 graduation list. See *Wichita Beacon,* May 18, 1952.

8. The first time Wong appears in the city directory as a cook at the T-Bone Club is 1959. See *Polk's Wichita City Directory,* 1959.

9. This anti-liquor law for dance and supper clubs had been in place since 1927. See "Order Dance Halls to Close at 12 P.M.," *Wichita Beacon,* February 8, 1939.

10. See also "Wichita Club Owner Sentenced," *Wichita Eagle,* January 9, 1960.

11. Wong's children were contributing their labor to the family economy; historically, Asian American children have played this critical role. See Yong Chen, "Invisible Historical Players: Uncovering the Meanings and Experiences of Children in Early Asian American History," in *Asian American Children: A Historical Sourcebook,* ed. Benson Tong (Westport, Conn.: Greenwood Press, 2004), forthcoming; Benson Tong, "The Worldview of Asian American Children," in ibid.

12. See also Wilma Mar Wong, telephone interview, conducted by Benjamine Matthei, March 15, 2003, transcript in editor's possession.

13. See also ibid.

14. See also ibid.

15. For an autobiography by a second-generation Chinese American who grew up in the 1950s that explores the negative reaction of his parents to interracial marriage in the family, see Ben Fong-Torres, *The Rice Room: Growing Up Chinese-American—From Number Two Son to Rock 'N' Roll* (New York: Hyperion, 1994). Although California's antimiscegenation statutes were declared unconstitutional in 1948, it was not until 1967 that all the other similar laws in other states were removed or lapsed from disuse. Sucheng Chan points out that, in spite of the longevity of the laws, and because few Chinese, Japanese, or Koreans were interested in marrying whites, these statutes "affected relatively few individuals." In sum, cultural prejudices, rather than legal obstacles, did more to proscribe such conjugal unions. See Sucheng Chan *Asian Americans: An Interpretive History* (New York: Twayne Publishers, 1991), 60–61.

16. See also Edward Mar Wong, interview, conducted by Teddie Barlow and Theresa St. Romain, March 7, 2003, transcript in editor's possession.

17. As part of the pre- to mid-1950s land reform in the countryside, the Chinese Communist Party weakened the old landlord elite by encouraging violent confrontations between landlords and other classes of the population. Probably one million or more people died during this phase of the revolution.

The lands of the landlord elites were seized and redistributed as part of the land reform. See Jonathan D. Spence, *The Search for Modern China*, 2d ed. (New York: W. W. Norton, 1999), 491.

Chapter 6: New Enterprises

1. See also Wilma Mar Wong, telephone interview.

2. The restaurant was featured in several newspaper articles, where the emphasis was on its popularity with local businesspeople. See Angelia Herrin, "Business Deals Born Over Tablecloths," *Wichita Eagle-Beacon*, February 23, 1981; quote in Jean Hays, "Breakfast These Days, It's Really Getting the Business," *Wichita Eagle-Beacon*, April 24, 1985.

3. Both Wilma and Edward Wong recounted the language difficulty and the general sense of isolation their mother experienced during the years they were growing up. See Wilma Wong, telephone interview; Edward Wong, interview.

4. Taco Tico was founded in Wichita in 1961, and expanded dramatically in the second half of the 1970s. By 1980 it had 140 stores in fifteen states. See "Taco Tico Cautious on Growth," *Wichita Eagle*, April 29, 1980. In 1983 a newspaper article reported that 52 percent of Wichita's estimated $140 million restaurant dollars were spent on fast food. See Nunzio Lupo, "Dining Dollar Goes to Fast Food," *Wichita Eagle-Beacon*, November 7, 1983. Clearly Wong was taking advantage of obvious trends in the restaurant industry.

5. Wong's 1983 trip to China and a brief biography of him are in Dick Dilsaver, "China Trip Adds Page to a Success Story," *Wichita Eagle-Beacon*, October 3, 1983.

6. See Robert M. Lee, "Journey to Ancestral Land," *Jingbao Journal* 54 (June–July 2001): 3–6.

Appendix

1. Michael Frisch, *A Shared Authority: Essays on the Craft and Meaning of Oral and Public History* (Albany: State University of New York Press, 1990), xxi.

2. Donald A. Ritchie, *Doing Oral History, A Practical Guide*, 2d ed. (New York: Oxford University Press, 2003), 35–36; see also David Lowenthal, *The Past Is a Foreign Country* (Cambridge: Cambridge University Press, 1985), 8.

3. Frisch, *Shared Authority*, 12.

4. David Thelan, "Introduction: Memory and American History," in *Mem-*

ory and American History, ed. David Thelan (Bloomington: Indiana University Press, 1990), ix.

5. Lowenthal, *Past Is a Foreign Country,* 208.

6. Ibid., 26.

7. Mary Paik Lee, *Quiet Odyssey: A Pioneer Korean Woman in America,* ed. with an introduction by Sucheng Chan (Seattle: University of Washington Press, 1990), 161–62; emphasis in original.

8. Lee, *Quiet Odyssey,* 160–61.

Index

WAYNE HUNG WONG is a retired businessman who lives in Wichita, Kansas. A veteran of World War II, he remains active in "Flying Tigers"–related veterans' organizations.

BENSON TONG is the author of *The Chinese Americans* (2003), and he has authored or edited other books on Asian Americans.

The University of Illinois Press
is a founding member of the
Association of American University Presses.

University of Illinois Press
1325 South Oak Street
Champaign, IL 61820-6903
www.press.uillinois.edu